Only Work Sundays

Only Work Sundays

A Laidback Guide to Doing Less
while Helping Your Church Thrive

Liz Miller

the pilgrim press

The Pilgrim Press, 1300 East 9th Street
Cleveland, Ohio 44114
thepilgrimpress.com

Printed on acid-free paper.

Library of Congress Cataloging-in-Publication Data on file.
LCCN: 2022948268

ISBN 978-0-8298-0027-2 (paper)
ISBN 978-0-8298-0028-9 (ebook)

MIX
Paper from responsible sources
FSC® C011935
FSC
www.fsc.org

Printed in The United States of America.

Dedicated to
the one who stuck me
in the corner with a book
while she attended committee meetings;
fed me leftover bread cubes
as she cleaned up communion;
and taught me to love
God and the church, in that order:
my mom.

Contents

Introduction

It is in vain that you rise up early
and go late to rest,
eating the bread of anxious toil;
for God gives sleep to her beloved.

Psalm 127:2

If I had the ability to choose a spiritual gift for myself, I would pick something really cool, yet appropriately biblical, like the ability to make miracles happen or prophesy about the future. Unfortunately, God didn't look at my Amazon wish list when crafting my gifts and I ended up with something a lot less desirable: the spiritual gift of laziness.

Laziness has an undue bad reputation. It conjures up images of a couch potato who has watched all of Netflix's original series but never read a book, or someone who keeps a long stick by their bed to flip off the light switch instead of getting up and doing it themselves. These behaviors might be ludicrous, but they're only one side of laziness. Laziness is also the ability to self-regulate. It prevents me from doing too much, too often to the detriment of my health and sanity. It keeps me from over-functioning, or when I do, it prevents me from doing it for long. My inner couch potato says, "Let's find a different way, perhaps an easier way, because this is not sustainable." (I bet you didn't know my inner lazy dude was so well spoken.)

For a long time, these traits did not feel like a gift; they felt like a character flaw. As a teen, I was placed in classes where the difference between the top performers and the rest of us was a singular, focused drive. I couldn't bring myself to be that driven—I always prioritized friends and a revolving door of extracurricular interests. I never let class deadlines get in the way of a good time and wondered where my classmates found the drive to pull all-nighters for the sake of completing assignments on time. In a moment of frustration at my unwillingness or inability to focus only on schoolwork, my mom once said, "It would be helpful if you could get just a little stressed out sometimes!" I rolled my eyes and returned to folding origami animals, my hobby du jour.

All of us are systematically programmed toward busyness. We celebrate herculean feats that seem to burst through normal concepts of time and reason. We champion those who push through pain and stress and discomfort in order to reach for greatness. We present ourselves publicly as people who do it all—at home, at work, at the gym—and leave out the parts where we quietly crumple into a heap on the floor because it's all a little too much. And when people do not fit that mold, we assign them labels like lazy. We tell them that instead of the work being too much, they are not trying hard enough.

Perhaps a better label is laidback: the commitment to slowing down and doing less, an unwillingness or inability to sacrifice yourself for the sake of outside expectations. When I made this switch in language, I began to see being laidback as countercultural instead of something that will only hold me down, especially professionally.

Embracing my laidback tendencies lasted until I started seminary to prepare for congregational ministry. Looking around at the practices and work ethic of my classmates, my professors, and my clergy mentors, I feared being too laidback would be my curse. Every clergy person I knew and respected was the opposite of laidback: they were overachievers. They spent most of their evenings at church meetings, maybe took one day off a week (which they would inevitably use to finish their Sunday sermon), and prided themselves on being involved in everything in their community. I wasn't sure how they did it, but I knew that if I was going to be a Good Pastor, I would need to learn how to do it too.

Seminary was the perfect training ground because in those three years there were always deadlines looming, never enough time to do the reading, and full course loads in addition to internships and community involvement. Occasionally a professor would make a passing reference to "self care," but we would knowingly roll our eyes because we knew that "self care" meant "falling behind."

It took concentrated effort and practice, but by the time I graduated seminary and began my first full-time ministry gig, I swore off my old slacker ways. I was ready to be the hardest working pastor that ever lived. My new church was ecstatic to welcome in a minister who was overflowing with energy and enthusiasm. I feasted on their approval and ignored my inner voice that warned me about taking on too much. I privately pledged to double down on my work ethic to make a good impression and become the Good Pastor I knew I could be.

In those early days I successfully performed the ideal version of my role. My sweet encouraging church loved my hard work, and the harder I worked, the more work they trusted me to do. It started a cycle where every affirmation I received spurred me to take on more and more. I remember thinking at the end of my first year: "This is not so bad! My workload feels full but balanced. I can do this!" I didn't realize that each subsequent year would mean adding more to my plate. Somehow, I made room for it all.

I stayed late redecorating the bulletin boards in the church school classrooms. I created programs from scratch, bringing a mix of theological research, creativity, and attentiveness to learning styles to build church programs that were not only engaging for participants but, more important to me, *original.* I wrote thank-you notes by hand and remembered birthdays. I volunteered for every committee and subcommittee that needed a spiritual adviser, and then at the first meeting, I volunteered to be the scribe or chair while everyone else shifted uncomfortably in their seats. Soon a common refrain at the end of the day, long after the rest of our staff had gone home, was, "You're still here?" Heck yes I was!

By my third year of ministry, I was exhausted. "My cup runneth over" felt more like a psalm of lament than a psalm of praise. I didn't know it yet, but I was also deeply depressed. I started going through my days in a fog. I had a difficult time concentrating on tasks or caring about outcomes. What little energy I had was spent trying to appear as if nothing were the matter because I did not have the ability or the language to express what was happening inside my head and body.

Many days if I went home for lunch—something I had always done quickly, returning to the office in less than an hour—I would crawl into bed and not leave it for the rest of the day. My wife would find me several hours later, still lying in bed in my work clothes. She became increasingly concerned about my mental health. It was the first time in my life I couldn't joke my way out of a situation. I canceled meetings, delegated tasks, and did the bare minimum I needed to survive and keep my job. I knew something was wrong with me. I knew something had to change, but I wasn't sure what.

Fortunately, I already had a therapist, and when I explained all that was going on, she recognized the telltale signs of depression and connected with my doctor who quickly got me on antidepressants. Over the next few weeks, it felt like the fog was lifting and I could look beyond myself, even as some of the symptoms of depression lingered. I was privileged to have the resources to triage the most urgent parts of my pain and quickly get back to "functioning human," but I required more than medicine to make changes in my self-destructive patterns. The built-up exhaustion required time to heal in addition to concrete changes in how I approached work.

During the months it took for the worst of the depression to lift, I did not share my pain with anyone other than my spouse and my doctors. Back at church, I could not bring myself to admit to the congregation, or even my colleagues, what I was going through. I had internalized unhealthy messages like "a pastor should take care of people, not be taken care of by them," or the more gruesome "don't bleed on your congregation; only show them your scars." I was afraid that if I admitted I needed help—for my health and at work—I would be judged, or worse, would no longer be considered fit for ministry.

When I was healed enough to return to (or close to) full speed, I was shocked to realize no one had particularly noticed that I was mentally and emotionally missing for a month. I had made excuses for the things I needed to miss and I had shown up for the essentials (like Sunday worship and youth group). But all those extra things? The extra volunteer work with committees and teams? The above and beyond programs that no one asked for? Showing up for every event in our community? Why didn't they notice I wasn't doing all those things?!

Instead of being relieved, my ego was bruised. I knew I needed to do less, but I also wanted people to miss me doing more.

Hadn't they expected me to be the best pastor ever? Hadn't they encouraged me to do more and more and more without asking what my limitations were?

As I sorted out this confusing flood of emotions, something weirder unfolded around me. I began to see that most of the balls I had dropped were picked up by other people, primarily church members. When I didn't volunteer to convene a group, someone else sent out a reminder email or gathered folks together. Church members met with each other about issues that came up in various programs and then looped me in via email. Members of our adult education team said to each other, "I have an idea…" and then the rest of the team supported them in making it a reality. All of the details I thought were my sole responsibility were organically being taken care of by other people, often better than I had done myself.

This moment was the beginning of a significant shift in the way I approached ministry. Over the following year, I consciously worked at letting go of those ideas of what a Good Pastor was supposed to do, and started focusing more on the areas I felt called to. Instead of being Team Captain I became Team Cheerleader, supporting and encouraging church members to also focus on the areas of ministry they felt called to, and letting them take the lead as often as possible. It was no longer my goal to be at the center of everything in the church. Instead, I strove to be in the background, shaping the work of the people around me gently and quietly as we worked alongside one another.

The more I encouraged my church leaders and volunteers to take ownership of our church's ministry, the more excited they were by my ministry. Affirmation stopped being "Wow, I can't believe you do all that!" to "Wow, thank you for supporting me in this work!" A weight had been lifted, and I finally felt like I was doing authentic pastoral ministry instead of performing the role of pastor.

There were other benefits as well. Because I wasn't at the center of everything, I started to have a meaningful life outside of the church. I became more involved in my hobbies, I had more time at home with my family, and I felt like each week included a true weekend off. It wasn't always perfectly balanced, but I slowly created healthy boundaries around my time that I didn't think were possible in congregational ministry. Through continued therapy and attention to my health, my depression faded into the background. Whenever it began to resurface, I was much better equipped at addressing it and making space to care for myself before it consumed me. I began to see that my younger laidback nature wasn't a curse but actually a gift that made my ministry more sustainable.

When I eventually moved from my first church to my current one, I took these newfound boundaries with me and strengthened them further. I made adjustments over the past decade of ministry and brought a great deal of experimentation to my work. What I've learned is that whether or not you are as naturally laidback as I am, there are concrete practices and leadership tricks that make it possible for any pastor to serve a church without feeling like ministry is consuming their whole life, or that they're neglecting their family, or sacrificing their personal health and wellbeing.

Not only is laidback ministry good for clergy, but it is also good for congregations. I've heard from other pastors who believe their congregations want to be The Best Church Ever. I reject this idea. When we look underneath the desire to be the best, we see the fear that our congregations have about no longer being relevant. We see a hunger for a way to make a difference in their community. There is no universal roadmap for churches on how to make an impact in the community or to fully live out their calling, so they turn to their pastor for guidance. Their pastor then internalizes a message that they have to be the one to do it themselves.

Our church members are just as stressed out and overworked as clergy. When you tell them they don't have to be the world's best church, that they can focus on what brings them joy and helps them find meaning, they most often breathe a sigh of relief. Our church members want to faithfully chill out as much as our clergy do.

Laidback ministry leaves church members more equipped to be the church no matter who is preaching in the pulpit, and it allows congregations to clarify who they are and what their unique gifts are as communities of faith. Laidback ministry allows churches to deepen what they are best at and free themselves of the guilt of continuing the things they feel like they have to do because they've always done it that way or because that's what Good Churches do.

I have served two churches with wildly different personalities but who are very much alive and thriving in their own ways. One is a multi-clergy congregation while the other is a solo pastor church with active lay leaders. They are both predominantly white. One is predominantly cisgender and straight while the other is a more diverse mix of genders and sexualities. They both have balanced budgets and an endowment to draw from in relatively sustainable ways, and both have leadership that feels like they could do "more" in every sense of the word if they just tried harder. They both look back on the glory days of church from forty years ago and wonder with prayerful hope what the next forty years will bring. These things matter and don't matter—your context might overlap in some ways and differ in others, but it helps you understand the environment in which these methods worked for me. This book will offer you guiding principles that can be applied to your specific circumstances, whether you are a huge rural congregation in the center of town or a tiny urban church looking for renewal.

My personal identity also matters. I am a white, genderqueer lesbian. I am a millennial, which used to mean I was a youth in the church but now means I am decidedly middle-aged. My race and gender and age play into how congregations receive me in the same way that all clergy's identities shape their leadership and how they are perceived. There are some things I can't get away with because I'm not a cis male, but there are many other things made easier because I am white. Again, you might overlap in some ways and differ in others in your own identities. It is important for each of us to understand how our identities impact our role in our own congregation.

Laidback ministry is for pastors who crave a different way to minister and have a life outside the pulpit, who long to reorganize their days so that they do not feel a huge chasm between work and home. It is for pastors who feel like the success or failure of their congregation rides on their shoulders and who wonder what their people would do without them. It is for pastors who want to take two days off each week without the weight of an unfinished to-do list over their head or without feeling guilty at not showing up to every community potluck.

For those who are willing to give up their addiction to busyness and move from the center to the sidelines of their congregation, I'm here to introduce you to laidback ministry. It's an approach to ministry that is playful but also requires communication, clarity, and commitment. Laidback ministry empowers committees and teams to work more effectively and uses vision setting to clarify a congregation's shared ministry. It cultivates collaboration with neighbors to lighten your workload. Most importantly, laidback ministry provides a sustainable framework to lean on during stressful seasons and periods of "I can't possibly keep going at this pace." Use this book to learn from my mistakes, experiments, and successes. Even if you don't possess the gift of being laidback, be inspired to try your own methods. Let's put on our pajamas, stretch out on the couch, and chill out together in the name of God.

Monday: The Philosophy

I was not prepared for the second day of being a pastor in my new church. The first day was easy; it was Sunday, a whirlwind of leading worship, meeting dozens of people, and eating sheet cake. By two in the afternoon I was back home and napping on my couch as my mind danced with the excitement and hope of all I had experienced in the sanctuary and the social hall that day.

The next morning, Monday morning, I walked past the empty sanctuary and social hall on the way to my office. I sat down at my new desk, turned on my computer, and waited. My calendar was as empty as the building around me. I felt like I should have Big Important God Business to take care of, but what was it?

Eventually, the Office Administrator came down to say good morning and remind me of the staff meeting at eleven in the morning. I checked my email and found four other requests for meetings waiting that I quickly scheduled for later that week. I called the church moderator and arranged to take her out to lunch sometime in the next few days. I looked through my desk drawers to see what treasures I had inherited from the previous pastor: a photo directory from thirty years ago, mimeographed brochures for the local funeral homes, and a dusty to-go communion set; nothing that told me what I should be doing with my time.

Someone knocked on my office door—a member who lived around the corner was out for a walk and wanted to say hi. We chatted for a while and they gave me a few names of elders who might appreciate a visit from their new pastor. After we said goodbye, I called those folks to make appointments to see them. At the staff meeting, I listened to all everyone else was doing with envy and made plans to meet with each staff person individually to hear more about their ministries.

By the time I started looking ahead to next Sunday's worship service, it was four in the afternoon and I was ready to go home. Between phone calls and emails, my calendar was full of visits and meetings for the rest of the week. I was relieved. I no longer had to wonder what I was supposed to be doing with my time. Everyone else had decided for me.

Thus began a pattern that would become so familiar that it took years to break. There was no manual on what a church pastor should do Monday through Saturday. We only ever talk about Sunday. This became a vacuum that other people were happy to fill, but the result was that eventually when I did figure out what I should be doing—looking ahead at upcoming seasons in the church, dreaming for future projects and reflecting on recent experiences, reading and researching emerging themes—there was no time left for it. My weekly schedule was shaped by what others needed and often felt like it was out of my hands. Things only began to change when I approached my week with intentionality and made space to focus on the work that helped me pastor and lead our church rather than simply react to everyone else's expectations and needs.

It took me several years to develop a sustainable, life-giving approach to ministry. I eventually started having conversations with colleagues where I realized my answer or outlook began deviating from the group norm. Friends would complain about how long it had been since they had a real weekend or vacation. Or someone might lament how it felt like their church needed them to do everything if anything was going to get done. As I shed patterns of over-functioning, I was increasingly uncomfortable treating the church like an adversary. I didn't want to brag about how poorly we clergy were taking care of ourselves as if it was a rite of passage on our way to martyrdom. Clergy often think of themselves as the ones who have to sneak in new ideas the way a parent might sneak vegetables into a toddler's dinner, but aren't we just as guilty? How much have we inherited from clergy before us or what messages have we absorbed about what it means to be a successful pastor or priest? When we ask each other how things are going, we start by saying, "I'm so busy!" as if to be any other way would mean you're not doing your job.

I often wonder if we stay in this cycle because it is the only option or because we get something out of it. For me it's a toxic combination of people pleasing instincts, conflict avoidance, and good old-fashioned ego. Even as I grew wary of the effects of overworking, something kept pulling me back into patterns that I knew were harmful and made me resentful of the institution that enforces them. We accept norms we would never allow for others, like poor boundaries around time and letting the weight of a whole organization lean on our productivity and creativity. Some of us thrive on being the center of church, and some of us are desperate to change but don't know where to begin. Either way, we need a different, more sustainable style of leadership.

As a pastor, I have been developing a laidback approach to ministry for a decade. It still feels like there are many days and some weeks where I am upside down with stress and feeling stretched too thin. There are whole seasons where it feels like everyone is in charge of my weekly schedule except for me. I'm not perfect; I'm a practitioner. I have fewer answers than I have wisdom to share about experiences that went spectacularly wrong for me. Ideas that worked in one setting might be a good fit in another congregation or might send you toward a different direction of your own. Laidback ministry is not about perfection. It is about knowing when to let go of control, having the tools to discern how something can be done and who can do it, and trying to get out of the way as much as possible.

This is a guide to help pastors reclaim the other days of the week. Sunday is the day when the church comes together as one body. You lead worship, you connect over a time of fellowship, and you might round out the day with visits, youth group, or meetings depending on your congregation's culture. It's a similar ritual each week not just for the pastor but for every staff member and lay leader. It's often a mystery to the congregation how their pastor spends their time the rest of the week. This is the story of how I reclaimed my week to be more proactive, more intentional, and ultimately how I learned to work less by getting out of my own way and empowering my congregation to share the work of ministry.

With a title like *Only Work Sundays*, it seems like the following pages should be filled with missives that require absolutely no work for the pastor but magically produce the benefits of a lighter, more balanced schedule. Perhaps you hope these pages contain several readymade doctor's notes to hand to your congregation excusing you from your most onerous duties like writing the monthly newsletter column, evening meetings that last until ten, or the annual all-weekend denominational gathering where Major Guest Speaker reminds you once again that the Church is in decline. Before you get any further into this book, I have to break your heart a little and be honest with you: initially it takes more work to ultimately do less.

There are practices to think through and shifts to be made in your work patterns upfront. It is going to require giving up some of the habits you're accustomed to and giving up the idea that you know what's best for your church. Only after that will the pacing and shared responsibility of living out your church's mission shift into new patterns. Together, with pastors and congregations working as partners, this book will help build a radical system of shared responsibility, discernment of mission, and being the church together. The synergy and intentionality of Sunday mornings will begin to flow into the rest of the week. That kind of intentional change takes both commitment and concentrated work.

This is not a "Do These Ten Difficult Things and You'll Find Success" kind of resource. I am sharing stories of shifts in behavior, patterns, and ideas that helped me live into collaborative ministry and leave my ego at the door. Some of my stories do not have happy endings, but all of them have powerful lessons learned. In walking through a week of ministry together, I invite you to question the way things have always been or the way you have always done things. Bring a curiosity for new idea, and openness to experimenting and trying on new practices.

WHAT LAIDBACK MINISTRY CAN DO FOR YOU

I have a deep and abiding passion for doing the least amount possible to achieve the maximum impact. I love teaching others how to do what some might call "my job" so that I can enjoy the non-job parts of my life. (And so church members can find fulfillment in living out their own call to serve God through the church, of course.)

Here are some of the tangible benefits this laidback leadership style has afforded me:

My baseline emotion for a day at work is joy.

Joy is easily accessible, and it takes a whole lot to bring me down to the level of "stressed out" or "overwhelmed." Overwhelmed only happens about once a year and requires a string of incidents like a tragic funeral, staff turnover, and the Easter banners being lost in the same week. Most often I look forward to the day ahead of me and am fulfilled by the different tasks I have to do. I am often told that joy radiates through my presence in meetings, in problem solving when the unexpected happens, and on Sunday mornings. I name this first because it has not always been a characteristic that people have associated with me, and it only came to the forefront when I started leaning into a more laidback approach.

I have to read the weekly church email newsletter to find out what is going on.

I make it a point to know as little as possible about what is happening in the church. Okay, that may be a slight exaggeration. I know the broad sweeping strokes, but it is often helpful to not know any more than that. I know exactly who to ask when I need more details, but not knowing has empowered the rest of the church to rely on each other and our communications systems instead of defaulting to "go ask the pastor." Not everything comes through my door or passes by my desk. Not every decision is cleared with me first. This means I'm not micromanaging our church life, and I get the opportunity to read our publicity like our new members and visitors do—from the perspective of someone who doesn't yet know what's going on. It's a win-win! And it's easier to convince church folks to read the newsletter when they know even the pastor has to read it to keep abreast of the latest news.

I have more hobbies than your grandparents.

I don't do them all at once, or all of them every week, but I have rotating interests in running, biking, swimming, quilting, weaving, crochet, magic tricks, ukulele, French horn, and playing euchre. I'm also low-key obsessed with my hyperactive dog who takes up significant time and energy each day. He is a hobby unto himself. The point is that I have an active life outside of the church, and that is before you include my spouse and friends, both of whom I love spending time with.

I hang out with my wife on a regular basis.

See above. My work life is not the only thing that has needed adjusting over the years. It turns out that relationships of all kinds are more likely to thrive when you spend quality time together on a regular basis. I learned this the hard way after saying yes to every commitment in my life before making time for the lifelong commitment I made to my spouse, assuming those fleeting moments in bed before going to sleep or the groggy hugs on our way out the door in the morning were enough to suffice. It's not perfect. Since we don't share traditional weekends, we have seasons where we have to renegotiate what time together looks like in order to make sure that we are spending enough of it together. But I spend more weekends at home doing all the day-to-day, blissful, family things I love than I spend at church commitments.

I volunteer outside of the church.

During my first few years in ministry, the biggest mystery to me was how all these dedicated church members held down jobs as insurance executives and teachers and doctors and still had time to offer to the church every week on committees, special projects, and youth group volunteers. There were over a dozen church members who gave up a week of their hard-earned vacation to drive in a cramped van, sleep on the floor of an un-air conditioned church, and do manual labor. They blew my mind, because my job took up so much time that I couldn't imagine giving more time to something that had nothing to do with work. Now my service on a volunteer commission has me knee-deep in local government, and I find myself spending entire weekends out of town doing justice work unrelated to the church, giving up the coveted Sunday vacation days for the privilege of doing it. I'm as bad as all those generous do-gooders who carve out time for their church even when it seems like there is no more time to give.

These five shifts have been life changing and sustaining. And these are just the benefits for myself as a pastor and as a human who desires a fully lived life. As clergy we are told that we have a vocation—one—and that it is ministry in the church. That makes our job our primary purpose in life. I disagree. We have many vocations. Just like anyone else, we're called to our families, our relationships, activities that offer us enrichment, and volunteer work that is fulfilling.

There are countless benefits to laidback ministry for our church systems and for the other leaders in the church: more collegiality, more sense of collaboration and shared responsibility, more ownership of the church's mission and who is responsible for living it out (spoiler alert: everyone is responsible).

It took me years to stop feeling guilty when I talk about how great my weekend was, or if I don't have a story to share about being overburdened or misunderstood or stressed to the max with my clergy colleagues. My hope is that it will take you less time and that together we will learn new ways of leading and revolutionize our work week.

"BOUNDARY" IS NOT A BAD WORD

The first thing that fades for me when I start to take on too much are boundaries with my time. Saying yes to too many new projects and responsibilities—even ones I am excited about—ends up having a trickle-down effect that impacts my emotional and spiritual well-being (I need down time to be my best self!) and my relationships (I am cranky and checked out when I'm doing too much). I have to build in accountability for myself long before that happens in order to mitigate my inevitable fall into over-commitment. When I practice carving out time every single week to non-ministry nourishment, this becomes a boundary that signifies the rest of my life is as valuable as my ministry. Here are some of the ways this has worked for me:

Have activities I love that are unrelated to church.

While working in my first church, I joined a weaving class that met every single Monday afternoon. It was an easy time for me to keep marked off on my calendar, and because I often had Monday night meetings, it ensured that I kept one part of that day for myself. Having the predictability of my Monday afternoons at the weaving studio helped me commit to it. When I started the class, I would just say I wasn't available if someone asked to meet on Monday afternoon. Eventually I started to name and claim my weaving class, knowing that I was just as deserving of two hours a week doing something I love as the next person is.

A colleague loved playing handbells, but instead of joining her church handbell choir (hello, that's pastoral care disguised as choir practice!), she joined a community handbell choir in the next town over where she could be as anonymous as she wanted. It is important to have a life outside of your church, something you are showing up for on a regular basis and engaging in that brings you joy. Pick up a hobby. Sign up for a class. Join a group.

I challenge you, if you do not have something that easily fits in the "life outside of ministry" category, to try new things. Classes and community are as close as the internet these days, so we are no longer limited to what is available at our local recreation center or required to take on hobbies that are cost prohibitive. Maybe an activity that involves other people, even if you are learning side by side, feels like too many people. What can you schedule for yourself that doesn't have to do with your job or Jesus? Set a goal for yourself before the end of this chapter. Do a search online and find something you are interested in. Put it on your calendar and then dive in.

Have a person who will keep me accountable.

The best thing I ever did was marry someone who is a truth teller and has strong boundaries around their time (among many other swoon-worthy qualities). My wife will not hesitate to let me know when I start to disappear into my work, and it's embarrassing to admit that I do not always have the self-awareness to recognize the signs on my own . . . but I don't. Did I already warn you that I have more failures than successes?

I'm a lot more self-aware than I was a decade ago, but I still benefit from having people who know me well enough to be honest with me and whom I respect enough to listen to. My wife is this person. My therapists and spiritual coach are these people. I have a few colleagues who keep me accountable (and vice-versa) and a few friends who don't understand clergy life but do understand enough to complain when I start piling on excuses as to why I can never hang out. I need people who expect honesty and integrity from me and whose relationships I value enough to prioritize and keep working at.

Who are those people in your life? Is it your mom who always says, "You work too hard" when you call her? Maybe that's not nagging but the voice of the Holy Spirit trying to get you to listen. Is it a therapist or coach? Is it a friend or a colleague, locally or online? Try asking someone to be an accountability partner—name your goals and what kind of check-in would feel supportive. Sometimes this kind of accountability happens organically, and sometimes we have to directly say aloud, "This is the support I need in this season of my life. Can you help?" What does it feel like to invite someone into your accountability?

Have rituals of personal reflection.

I am envious of people who fill calendars and journals with daily and weekly reflections, tracking goals and tweaking to-do lists as they go. I am not that person. I have more to-do lists than I have items on them, spread across the first pages of otherwise empty notebooks, on sticky notes at home and in my office, and in every organizational app that the App Store offers. That kind of purposeful organization or self-evaluation does not work for me. I channel what little discipline I have into other areas of my life like creating and following workout schedules (because that gets me out of the office!)

What I excel at is pausing in the moment, particularly the moment when I feel overwhelmed and stressed to the max. I wrap myself in a blanket like a burrito and ask, "How did I get here?" Then I look back on my week with an honest (but not shame-filled) lens and imagine how I might make different choices in the next week. I sit with myself until what feels overwhelming and impossible breaks down into bite-sized pieces with alternative realities. I sit until I can breathe deeply again and the stress feels like it is beside me, not within me. Spontaneous reflection is reflection. It works for me. And because I do it when something inside me is longing for it, it's not another deadline or expectation on my calendar that I've missed.

What does self-reflection and personal evaluation look like for you? How do you look back on your week and use that information to inform what comes next? Is this a daily ritual or something that happens when you recognize the signs of needing it? Do you write it down, speak it out loud, or simply listen to your own inner voice?

EXCUSES, EXCUSES, EXCUSES

Every congregation is different, but regardless of your theology, polity, or context, every congregation has three things they love more than anything else: God, service, and proclaiming, "But that's the way it's always been done!" We have dozens of variations of this phrase that we toss around without realizing it. When we are asked to try something new or experiment, we're quick to name why it won't work or poke a hole in the idea. Here are some of the protests I've heard about why an easy breezy clergy lifestyle just won't work:

Being workaholics is just the way pastors are!

Is it, though? It intrigues me that so many professions come with stereotypes about the type of work environment or type of people that are drawn to them. Artists are flighty and unreliable. Accountants prefer numbers to humans and are antisocial. Clergy are workaholic, holier than thou types. But what about my cousin who is a professional designer at a major company and runs her own independent print business on the side? She is more organized and structured than anyone I know. And what about my old accountant friend who was the life of the party? You couldn't take her anywhere without her making a new friend.

If stereotypes are just stereotypes, can we imagine a different kind of clergy person? One who has love for their church and love for themselves when they say, "I want to find a time to meet with you, but I'm not available Thursday nights. I have my cycling group." One who says, "This is a great idea, but the truth is I don't have enough bandwidth to lead it right now. Can we brainstorm together who might be the right leader?" A pastor who practices boundaries as well as vulnerability, who leads with the fullness of their humanity and understands in their bones that even though they were called to serve their church, it is just one of many callings that has a hold on their life.

My congregation expects more of me, not less.

There is a myth about congregations wanting to suck the life out of their ministers. The problem is that most congregants have never heard this myth and would be horrified if they thought it was being perpetuated about them. I am willing to believe there might be real life churches where this is true, but I also believe they are very much in the minority of congregations. What fuels this idea that clergy are never enough or that congregations want more? Anxiety. Anxiety from both church members and pastors about what the perfect congregation looks like, who they are called to be, and how they will measure up against the giant shadow of the ordained saints who came before them.

It is also fueled by fear. Fear of claiming who we are today and believing that is enough. How many of us are clinging to the church from decades past? When families had one parent at home with dozens of hours free to volunteer at the church each month and congregations were generously staffed? How many of us are, consciously or unconsciously, trying to meet the expectations and output of the church from yesteryear?

What would it look like if we embraced where we are and reset expectations through honest communication, vulnerability, and hope for a future that is grounded in reality? What if our conversations about how God is calling us to be the church didn't start with a retrospective of the history of all the church has done, but instead began with the gifts and strengths that the people in our pews today bring, including the pastor?

I'm too tired. I can't handle one more thing.

If you find yourself muttering this over your third pot of coffee for the day, burnout isn't a distant neighbor, but has moved in and taken up residence. Putting in some initial effort will actually result in several fewer things to do. I promise. And if you are in the painfully familiar place of feeling overwhelmed, like you will burst if one more person asks you for something or one more unexpected email arrives in your inbox, please reach out for help. Call a therapist or coach. Call a friend or colleague. Call your church president, head deacon, or chair of your support committee. Call someone you can trust and say, "I can't carry this by myself. I need help."

This life is exhausting and that's before we try to be a disciple of Christ in an organization where everything—from the way we communicate to who is in our pews—is changing fast. If you're too tired to consider changes that can have profound effects on your ministry, maybe this isn't the right time. The first stage of change is pre-contemplation, where we think about new ideas or ways of being long before we have the words to verbalize them. There is no requirement to rush through or implement ideas. Some seasons are about putting your head down and continuing on to survive. I've been there. I'll be there again. And if that's you right now, that's okay.

My prayer for you is that this season is just that—a season—and that soon you will find yourself in a different place. I pray that you take the time for rest and restoration where you can find it. I pray that when you are ready to imagine a different way of being, you will have inspiration from this resource, and hand out copies to members of your church to study with you, as you begin again.

Church members are not oblivious to the conflicting feelings and massive amounts of stress that their pastor carries. Like many clergy, whenever I meet someone on the plane, train, or checkout line, they want to tell me about their faith journey. And if they are actively involved in a church, what they usually share is something like, "Reverend So-and-So works too hard. I hope we don't burn them out. I hope they don't leave." Or sometimes they will share, "I want to support my pastor, but I don't always know how. I wish there was a way we could take some of the stress from them."

Clergy Friends: whether or not we realize it, our humanity is showing, in all its imperfections. Our congregations notice all that we do, and all that we struggle with. They don't always have the words to tell us. Sometimes they think that by keeping it to themselves they are protecting us or respecting our position and authority. But they notice, and guess what? Our congregations are longing to work with us to sustain our tenures, to strengthen the whole ministry of the church, and to move the barometer from The Pastor's Church to Everyone's Church.

WHAT WOULD JESUS DO? (PROBABLY A MIRACLE OR SOMETHING ELSE ABOVE MY PAY GRADE)

When we talk about Jesus, we tend to focus on the flashier side of his ministry: miracles, memorable sayings, and meals. There is another key element that flows throughout his whole ministry: rest. Jesus rested up on a mountainside, with and without his closest companions, in a desert, and sleeping on a boat. Jesus knew how to take a timeout and replenish himself with rest and prayer. Rest and prayer were often linked together, prayer coming only during times of rest. Coincidence? I think not.

When we study the Gospels, the part about rest either ends up as a footnote or drops off all together. Today we're more likely to reference Jesus resting frequently as an admonishment (just another thing you're failing to do), not as encouragement or an inspiration. Jesus resting might be featured in a sermon on individual self-care but often doesn't dig deeper and doesn't address systemic practices that lead to burnout.

When Jesus goes away from the crowds to rest, they don't stop being a crowd. They don't stop having needs. The ministry he was working to build didn't just pause. Those disciples and followers who had been listening and learning would be activated in those moments. Jesus is about teaching, right? An important part of teaching is modeling, stepping back and letting someone try for themselves, and then offering feedback. This is the model Jesus exemplifies. The "work" is still happening when he goes away, but he allows someone else to implement and lead day to day.

The writers of the Gospel focused on Jesus's ministry, but he was focused on equipping disciples. It wasn't him doing everything until he died, handed over the reins, and circled back once for feedback post-resurrection. The disciples are sent out early on to spread the word of God on behalf of Jesus. He equips them to do their work when he is not present. He does not say, "Stick close to me, I've got this covered." He tells them they need to reach more people and more towns than any one person could possibly get to. If we take that model of ministry seriously, we should be getting out of the way as often as possible, trusting the people in our congregations that have been called to this work, and preaching that it takes more than one person. Jesus going out to rest gives others an opportunity to step up and lead.

I'm not drawing this analogy to equate clergy with Christ and church members with disciples, which happens too often and creates unhealthy expectations. We are all disciples together called to follow Christ. We're all part of the flock. We're all ministers, called by God to care for our neighbors and creation. The more I separate myself from the rest of the flock, the more I turn into a wolf who is unable to see that Christ is the head of the church, not me. We've all been sent out to serve together. The pastor might be telling a story while a resident social worker helps connect someone with needed resources and a tender-hearted youth holds space for one who is grieving. We can learn from what Jesus did and do likewise without separating ourselves using power and authority of an ordained status. That's how we got into the trouble of clergy feeling like they had to do everything themselves in the first place.

My favorite example of what happens behind the scenes when Jesus rests happens right after he and the disciples feed the great crowd with just a few fish and loaves of bread. This was his busy season of work. Hundreds, if not thousands, of people would have been newly inspired, attuned, and ready to commit themselves to his movement of love and compassion. I can imagine the energy he would have felt from the crowds, and the exhaustion that would also be present as he navigated a multitude of needs and personalities, trying to teach his disciples how to be leaders in this work alongside him.

The crowd's needs and hunger would have felt urgent, but the need for rest in the midst of such great demand was also urgent. Jesus sends his disciples to the boat while he wraps things up with the crowd and tells the disciples he will meet them on the other side. Then, he goes up on a mountain to pray alone. When he sends the disciples off on their own to make the next journey, he is assuring them that he trusts them. They don't need Jesus to guide them every step of the way. I imagine this is his way of telling them that if they arrived on the other side and he isn't there yet, they know what to do without him. They have been equipped.

Instead, before the disciples can reach the other side, the weather gets wild and the boat gets tossed by the waves. The storm is unexpected, and the disciples don't know what to do in rough weather. Jesus realizes the disciples are in trouble on the boat, so he leaves his place of rest to guide them to safety.

Jesus was not wrong to leave the disciples. It was not inevitable that his rest would be interrupted by a crisis. He took time away and when he was truly needed, he returned, probably a lot more ready to be present and pastoral than if he had not taken that time to himself. Much to my surprise, Jesus doesn't sigh as he gets up to go save them. He does not mumble and mutter on the way, and he does not chastise them when he arrives. He simply says, "Take heart, it is I; do not be afraid" (Matthew 14:27b).

This is a model for how a faith community could be. We could each be empowered to live out our specific calls in community, completing our tasks and doing the work of being the church in different ways, including taking time to step back for rest or prayer while others take care of what needs to be done. Then, if/when someone needs our help, we come to their assistance and provide encouragement. We don't all have to be in the boat together all the time. There is a lot to do. Some people have to pass out food, manage the crowds, or prepare for the next event, and some people need a break. Through it all, God is sending the Holy Spirit to guide us back together to remind each other to take heart and be not afraid. When an entire team or congregation embraces their shared ministry and different tasks, there is less to fear.

The Gospels show us that rest is important for rest's sake and for the sake of our spiritual lives, but it is also important because when one person rests or a small group takes a time out, others are able to keep living out the mission, living into their ministry, and taking a turn at guiding the boat. As a pastor, often our job is to encourage and empower our fellow disciples, helping them step into their gifts and bringing people together to serve. With clarity on what our role is and isn't, and a resounding call to rest along the way, we are ready to incorporate a more laidback ministry into the rest of our workweek. Let's begin!

Tuesday: Creating the Vision

Recently, I was in a team meeting with a focus on church programming for the year ahead. We looked back at our events for previous years and realized that we always* do an all-church book read. Choosing a new read for the coming year seemed like an easy place to begin. People started listing off all the best books they had read in the last few months, everything from *New York Times* best-selling fiction to local authors to topical non-fiction books. I developed a huge reading list for myself

* Always meaning that it had not been for so long that we couldn't remember a time before it, but that it had definitely been for more than one year.

based on everyone's recommendations, but after twenty minutes of throwing out ideas we were no closer to deciding a book for the year.

Instead of accomplishing our task, the energy drained out of the room and we started to feel overwhelmed. How was this group of book lovers supposed to choose one selection when each option promised to be life-changing, spirit-lifting, and soul-saving? We didn't know how to move forward on a simple book read, let alone planning a whole year of programs. I began to sense that this meeting was going to stretch late into the night as the dodging decisions dance commenced.

Finally, a lone voice spoke up, asking, "What is our goal for the all-church book read?" I blinked as if staring at the sun breaking through thick clouds. No one had mentioned a goal; we were too busy peddling our favorite authors to each other. They continued, "What is our purpose with this event other than that we always do it? Should we connect it to a larger theme? What do we want people to get out of it? Maybe having a goal will help us make a decision."

Suddenly the room became energized and our conversation shifted from picking a book to exploring what we wanted to get out of this program. Understanding the broader hopes for continuing this tradition made the selection much easier. Once we clarified our intentions, it only took a few minutes for the decisions to fall into place. We discovered that to move forward we had to slow down and step back.

A key part to freeing yourself from overworking is getting clear about the work you, and by extension your congregation, are called to do. Sometimes it feels like we vacillate between "we've always done this" and the "newest and greatest church trend" without having a concrete vision for what kind of church we are called to be at this time or what specific kind of ministry we are called to do together. Having a vision that all parts of the congregation understand and embrace, and concrete goals that you are working toward together, acts as a helpful boundary that frees you from being the church of all things or running yourself ragged trying. Call it goal setting, visioning, objectives, purpose—whatever language we use, it is often the first thing we set aside in the work of the church. For all the enjoyment we get from proposing new ideas or putting dates on the calendar, we are left feeling like hamsters running on a wheel with no way to get off and no destination to reach.

Without a shared vision across church leadership or the congregation as a whole, the pastor becomes the one who creates and maintains the vision. This is a recipe for burnout. When one person is the keeper of a vision for the whole organization, suddenly everyone is looking to one person to know what they should be doing. The result is that the person needs a steady supply of brilliant ideas to feed the vision, and if that one person takes a breather or steps back, the whole effort collapses. No thank you! I don't need that kind of pressure! Laidback ministry invites us to share the workload with the whole church, including the work of dreaming new dreams, experimenting with new ideas, and discerning the future of the church. We're not just trying to hand off the tasks we already have. We're working together to build something that is sustainable regardless of who is serving in what role.

We have all been a part of visioning processes that felt so abstract and lofty that we question how it relates back to regular people who are looking for concrete ways to experience community or dig deeper into their faith. In fact, that may be exactly the association that comes up when we hear the word "visioning." Vision statements are full of beautiful language but often feel disconnected from the day-to-day life of the church. You don't always need to start with a fancy, flowery vision statement. Sometimes it just takes someone asking, "What are we doing here? What is our goal?" to help reorient a group's direction toward something that feels like it has a clear purpose or fits a larger vision for the congregation.

BIBLICAL BLUEPRINT

Hebrew prophets, Jesus, and other old-timey leaders were all about setting forth a vision. After all, what were those prophets doing? They were the original visionaries. Here's how they did it:

They listened to and talked with God.

They cultivated a deep understanding of who God is and who God called them to be. Pausing to listen to God is about rest, but it's also about active discernment of what comes next and where God is calling us to go.

They made a point to include other people in setting the vision.

We call this an assessment. Prophets took stock of who would be impacted by what is to come—their neighbors, their congregations, their wider community, or a specific part of that community. They might do a congregational survey, like in Exodus and Numbers, where we read chapter after chapter of the Israelites' complaints in the wilderness. We interpret this as whining, but in the context of vision setting, I like to think of it as constructive feedback. When the Israelites vocalized what they were unhappy with, it allowed Moses and Aaron to assess the group's emotional and spiritual readiness for change, and as leaders it helped them shape the next steps in their people's journey.

Prophets shared God's visions with everyone, everyone, everyone.

They were not quiet about their visions. They shared their visions with people who agreed with them and people who didn't agree with them, to apathetic individuals and folks who only came around when fishes and loaves were being distributed. Jesus was especially talented at reminding everyone of the vision of God's kingdom here on earth and how every person was called to be a part of it. Think about those parables we still love to unpack and ponder. Parables are different ways of sharing God's vision using language that each group Jesus encountered would have understood, whether they were lawyers or tax collectors or fishermen. You know who else did this? Paul, in his letters to each of his congregations. Every letter he writes includes a passionate, "Don't you remember we agreed to do this? I thought we were on the same page! C'mon people!" When we have a vision, we are called to share it, and keep sharing it, until it is woven into the fabric of the church.

Prophetic leaders do this work over and over again.

It's not a onetime process, and it's not always linear. A big part of ministry is holding the vision out in front of the congregation, tweaking it as it needs to change, listening to God, and reminding folks of their part in creating the vision. We might do all of these things in one day or one worship service. We might do a deep dive into different parts of a vision across a whole season or year of ministry. Often, we put the most emphasis on the creative work of setting the vision, but our day-to-day mission is in carrying it out and assessing where our folks are at any given moment. This process is shared across the congregation. Different people, whether they are clergy or lay leaders or staff, keep the vision in view and remind the congregation of it through their specific roles in the church. Our shared vision is an integral part of the life of the church.

WHAT KIND OF VISION?

Congregations simultaneously work toward short-term visions and long-term visions. We might create a strategic plan every ten years, but there are many small visions that feed into the bigger picture. Those short-term visions create wins and feel-good moments that compel us onward and help us tackle the longer, harder, more nebulous long-term work.

A long-term vision or strategic plan should be a living document that is adapted and referred to frequently. The plan itself is useless if it is not an active part of the life of the church. It should be relatable enough that it can be translated into different spaces, whether it is a brainstorming meeting with a ministry team, a liturgy in worship, or an experiential lesson in church school. It should be easy enough to interpret that when lay leaders or staff transition, a new group can pick it up and continue the work without wondering what was intended or calling the previous pastor to ask things like, "What does 'formulate a growth opportunity for emergent and divergent ministries' mean?"

Long-term visions are cultivated and embraced by the congregation as a whole. This is the work that emerges out of all-church retreats, dedicated discernment time, and ongoing conversations, feedback, and buy-in. A congregation's deepest hopes, grounded in their strengths and the opportunities before them, are the foundation for a long-term vision. When that is the foundation, excitement ensues. A prayerful process, or an understanding of how God is at work in the congregation should also be a part of it.

The motions that my congregation brings to our congregational annual meeting tend to transform into our long-term visions. They vote to affirm ideas and projects that speak to their deepest values or represent a significant spiritual or financial investment. Projects have ranged from a multiyear commitment in expanding our model for service trips to affirming our ministry as a climate justice congregation to investing in practical but lifesaving safety projects in our physical buildings. By the time each one came before the congregation, the vote was mostly symbolic because everyone had participated in prayer and discernment, discussions and planning, and the proposed vision had drawn on their input and ideas.

Long-term visions should not be based on something the congregation is lacking or believes they need to change in order to be a "successful" church. When you set a vision based on a deficit or something that needs a total makeover, you are setting up a dynamic that will ensure you feel not good enough or like you are being chastised for the next five to ten years. There is a reason the Tenth Commandment says, "Thou shall not covet thy neighbor's youth group or average worship attendance or feeding ministry." We want to start a visioning process from a foundation we already have in place. Instead of asking, "What are we missing that will make us the best church ever?" Look around and ask, "What is unique about our church or what is working well that we might expand on?"

Smaller or short-term visions allow us to focus on one theme for a season without feeling like we are reinventing the church's identity or talking about the same thing so long that it loses meaning. A short-term vision might be spending one year exploring and living into a Bible verse or sacred story. It might be inviting the public to experience hospitality by hosting a community festival or passing on a worship ritual from one generation to the next. It might be pointing out something the church does really well like welcoming new visitors without overwhelming them and finding ways to intentionally celebrate it together.

Short-term visions are more like low stakes experiments. They are opportunities to play and try on new ideas without committing to a particular outcome. A short-term goal might be proposed as a learning lab: what will we learn about ourselves if we try this initiative or focus on this theme or live into this value for a set amount of time? Approaching them with an ethos of play creates a burst of energy or newness that generates other ideas or gives a congregation the feeling of being united with a common goal.

These small, meaningful moments happen constantly in communities of faith, but many of them happen without being recognized as visions for the church, connected with our values, and tied to larger goals we have. When we treat them as independent projects without tying them into the wider story of the church, we create more work for ourselves (ugh) because we are constantly reinventing the wheel instead of learning from our experiments, reflecting on their success or impact, and building on them in future endeavors.

These short-term visions become intentional when we name what is happening, articulate our vision, and evaluate their impact when they are over. My church did this at the beginning of the COVID-19 pandemic when folks longed to connect with each other but most of us were not venturing far from home. We divided the whole congregation into small neighborhood groups and provided ideas for the ways their group could connect with each other. Our lay leaders introduced this opportunity as part of the larger vision of our COVID-19 response as well as an ongoing vision we were exploring around the ways we are called to love our neighbors. Grounding it in a wider story encouraged folks who might have been hesitant to give it a try. We launched fifteen groups that summer but only one of them fulfilled the vision by becoming an ongoing cohort—the other groups faded after one or two gatherings.

The easiest thing would have been to write this idea off as mostly unsuccessful, but instead we reached out to the congregation—those who had participated and those who chose not to. We asked them about their experience and what they would do differently if they were in charge of the initiative. We talked to the group that gelled and asked why they thought they had a different result from the others. We listened not knowing what we would do with the information but hoping it would help us at a later date.

Almost two years later we heard the same need: desire to connect with small groups of people and a longing to stay close to home. We pulled out the feedback we gleaned from our original neighborhood groups and totally revamped the program.

This time most of the groups found the connections they were longing for and the feedback we received was overwhelmingly positive. Many participants did not know these groups were born out of the earlier effort, but we needed that first experiment to enable our leaders to learn, evaluate, and create the formula that worked the second time.

When we say yes to trying a new idea in our church, we should share an understanding that it is tentative and experimental, maybe even playful, instead of becoming quickly invested in a particular outcome. It is important to listen to each other and check in with leaders about how an initiative is working out in practice rather than when it was just a hypothetical discussion, and what adjustments need to be made or if a different direction needs to be explored.

SETTING THE VISION

If you ask eighty church members what their big idea for the church is, you are likely to get eighty responses. If you ask the pastor, they will add eighty of their own ideas. Is this sounding a bit like that book discussion planning meeting my church had? Exactly. We've all been in that meeting. When church leaders and pastors are thinking about the visions and goals they have for their congregation, their primary role is to listen to those eighty ideas and find the common threads. You should be listening so much and so often that it feels like you are spending an entire day each week just listening to people and their ideas, hopes, dreams, fears, and failures concerning the church.

Opportunities to gather intel about where people are at or what they are longing for are endless. Notice what parts of your sermon get a hearty "Amen!" and what parts are met with crickets. What does that tell you about the people in the pews and what they respond to? What are people sharing with you in the handshake line after worship or what articles, other church newsletters, and social media posts are they sending your way?

Where do committee meetings get energized and what topic always feels like it sucks the wind out of the room?

My church's council has a "comment corner" that is printed in every bulletin and provides space for people to write their ideas, their gripes, and their questions. Sometimes the comments just say that the pew pencils need to be sharpened, but other times someone asks a question that becomes the beginning of a vision for the church's next great project. An idea written in a comment is taken to council to be discussed. They might share it with other teams, one of which might say, "We've been exploring this very idea! Maybe this is a sign we should continue the conversation." Or in another scenario a team might say, "We talked around and around this idea for three years but couldn't match our congregation's gifts and resources with bringing it to life." Either way, tell that person they aren't alone in dreaming up that idea.

Sometimes listening is about hearing what isn't there. When we put out an idea and no one responds, that shapes the larger vision because it lets you know that although it might be a good idea, it's not the right time or it's not for that congregation. Some of my congregation's best clarity of mission and purpose has come from listening to our no's, trusting that God speaks to us in the no's as well as the yes's.

One example from my experience is when my congregation, who is vocal about immigration rights, became horrified in 2016—2017 at what was happening with the US's deportation practices with our southern border. Church members started asking if we could become a sanctuary congregation for immigrants threatened with deportation. The sanctuary movement has been around for decades but gained new traction across the country as congregations longed to be able to do something to make a difference in their own community to someone who might need help.

When the question of becoming a sanctuary congregation was informally raised a few times by different folks, I started asking around if our church had ever explored that idea before. I asked folks who had been in the congregation a long time because I was surprised that we were not already a sanctuary congregation—this was right in our social-justice-loving, public-stand-taking wheelhouse. I asked our racial justice team. I asked our justice and peace team. It took listening to the stories people told to find out that we had explored becoming a sanctuary congregation very early on in the movement but had never moved forward. A conflict emerged during the process, the details of which I still don't understand, that was more symbolic of the conflict avoidance of that era of the church than of the particular issue of supporting immigrants needing sanctuary.

Twenty years later there was some excitement or sense of urgency to undertake this work, but there was also reluctance at the memory of that earlier conflict. We had since grown as a congregation in our ability to sit in conflict and work through painful situations, but memories are powerful and have a way of collapsing time. I wanted to push the congregation forward, but I kept brushing against some resistance. I also knew that this was not the only way to support immigrants, and perhaps because of the significant commitment it takes, should not be the first step in getting the congregation to show up for immigration rights.

Church leaders felt a sense of urgency and obligation because we had a building that was reasonably setup to accommodate a family: we have a bathroom with shower, washer and dryer, full kitchen, and a space for private living quarters. But you can't back your way into a vision. We kept listening for things like energy levels, community partners, long-term sustainability, and identifiable leaders who could take on this project. We listened further into the community in our quest to answer the question: is this a real need or is it a desire born of headlines?

Around the corner from us, a neighboring church went through the same listening process we did. Unlike our process, which raised more questions than answers, they had a clear vision: they were called to become a sanctuary congregation. They needed community partners who would support them if they were matched with a family, recognizing that they might need more resources or volunteer hours than their congregation could sustain. That fit our congregation's capacity and vision perfectly. We quickly and enthusiastically signed on to be a supporting partner in their vision to become a sanctuary church. Our neighbors did introduction sessions with us that clearly explained the commitment they were taking on and what they were asking from us as a supporting partner. They invited us to join them in their preparatory work by educating ourselves about the specifics of immigration communities in our area and learning more about the advocacy nonprofits who were our local justice leaders. We learned about what housing a family looks like from the big picture to the day-to-day reality and discerned what kind of volunteers we might provide if needed: gathering supplies, being present at their church, and advocating to local officials—whatever was needed to support them and the family they were serving.

Did I spend a few days feeling like our neighbor was the cooler church because they got to hold the press conference and be the ones proclaiming themselves a sanctuary congregation? Of course! I wanted all the glory for my people (and myself). But I also breathed a sigh of relief: our congregation was not ready to make that kind of commitment, no matter what that said about us. The damage we could do to someone's real life in their most vulnerable moment was too great to rush into the decision. And our wider community is such that it barely needed one sanctuary location, let alone two churches half a mile apart. Partnering together allowed the need to be met with each congregation living into their call to support immigrants in our own ways.

It deepened our commitment to immigration advocacy without rushing the formation of a vision. It took listening to the no's, to the reluctance, resistance, and hesitation, to find our way to a yes that was both about us and about a vision God had for our wider community.

LIVING OUT THE BIG PICTURE IN THE DAY TO DAY

The biggest challenge in keeping my congregation's vision front and center is balancing the big picture dreams with the reality of having to make broad-ranging day-to-day decisions. These include programs that will take place this month, ideas that have time sensitive answers, and unexpected enthusiasm that church members express for ministry proposals that may or may not fit our vision. The more I fall into old patterns and become the gatekeeper for the church's vision, the more likely I am to feel overwhelmed by all the micro-decisions that go into supporting a long-term vision or the more I am likely to stop intentionally cultivating short-term visions along the way.

When a church member comes to me with a new idea they have, it is not my role to approve or reject their proposal. It is my role to equip and empower them to go to the appropriate committee that will discern how it fits into our church's vision. I also have a role in equipping and empowering that committee to do their discernment work, but it should be clear to all involved that they are the decisionmakers and I am their cheerleader. Equipping and empowering is a lot less work than making decisions. Laidback ministry advocates for asking a group "What do you think?" rather than delivering a twenty-minute presentation about what I think.

The way this works in ministry for me is that a church member will come to me and say, "I would like our church to host a circus. It will be a great outreach to the kids in our neighborhood." No matter what I think about this idea, I don't want to squelch this member's enthusiasm. I get to be the yes person as I lead them to the group that will actually discern if we can fit a trapeze in the social hall. I can ask questions or add to their ideas, but ultimately the decision is not up to me.

I don't want to be the one to approve or deny new ideas because that would slowly shift our church's shared vision to my own. Our ministry teams represent the core ministries of our congregation—things that are central to who we are and what we do as a church. They represent areas such as worship, education, fellowship, and advocacy. Each of our ministry teams represents a piece of our church's overall vision. Their activities or focuses will inevitably shift over the years, but we believe we will always have some form of worship, some form of education, some form of fellowship. They have a better grasp of whether the circus is similar to something we are already doing, whether there might be energy to host a circus, or whether the circus might be interesting but the timing not quite right.

CONGREGATIONAL DISCERNMENT TOOL

Because our ministry teams mostly meet independently, it is helpful to have a universal tool that directs all of our teams toward the larger vision of the church and clarifies the ideas that they are trying on. My church leaders developed a discernment tool after an honest conversation between church leaders, lay and staff alike, where we admitted that we sometimes struggled to say no to someone's new idea. We all wanted to support each other and didn't want to risk hurting someone's feelings if their idea didn't become a reality or wasn't the next great hit in the church.

By developing a tool that helps us in our discernment, it gave us a way to set boundaries around our yes's and gave us a way to explain our decisions to others. It not only helped us make decisions, but it moved the larger visions of the congregation into the center of that decision making process—it wasn't about the whim or passions of the team making the decision, but the team was in prayerful conversation with the vision and passion of the whole congregation.

These graphics represent the three parts of our discernment process: What, How, and Who. Our first step is to make sure we understand WHAT the project is. What priority does it reflect? What other projects are we currently tackling or dreaming about in that priority? Is the goal of this new project already being met somewhere else in that priority?

Our congregation—through surveys, whole church discussions, and ongoing discussion by our Council—has identified three priorities of ministry we are called to do: healing, service, and advocacy. Your church might have different priorities or different categories that are most important. We certainly do other things, but the new programs or the big ideas we throw our energy into come back to these three priorities—they are what gives us energy, where we find our purpose, and are a big piece of our long-term vision. Every new proposal that a team tries on goes through the filter of these three priorities.

Once an idea is identified as fitting one of our three overall priorities, we start to imagine HOW this idea or project will come to life through two lenses: labor and finance. Labor envisions what kind of volunteer and staff energy will be needed to execute and sustain this project. What other projects are these leaders already engaged in and how will adding a new project impact their ability to serve on their previous project? Pro-tip: it's most helpful to involve those specific leaders in the conversation rather than talking about them or making assumptions. It's easy to either overcommit someone or assume they don't have time for something when they are longing to be asked. If there is not a clear pool of people to lead this, how will we find those people?

Labor also asks the question of what kind of engagement this project will require or produce: head (will we be learning something new together like you might in a book discussion or hosting a speaker series for the wider community?), hands (will we need people to physically volunteer their time and bodies to accomplish a task together like working in a fundraiser booth or spending a week building houses?), and heart (will people grow spiritually together like on a parenting retreat or a Lenten series on forgiveness?)

After we ask our labor questions, we move to finance. This order is intentional because if we are vibing with an idea, we tend to get more creative about funding. If we haven't fully tried on an idea, we're more likely to default into saying we can't afford it. So, if we're still talking about and trying on the idea by the time we get to finance, we have a lot of creative questions we can ask. How does this fit into our existing church budget or what teams might work together to fund it? Does it require additional fundraising, and will we ask our members or seek support from the wider community? Are there grant opportunities we can seek to fund this or partners in the community with whom we can work together, who have deeper pockets than we do? Asking questions of finance is not meant to be a barrier. It is a reality check as well as a question to activate our imaginations. If an idea or project truly fits a church's vision, I have heard folks say, "We believe in this so we will work to find the money." When that happens, it's a gobsmacking, jaw-on-the-floor, Holy Spirit blessing.

The final questions we ask are about WHO will be involved and who will be impacted by this project. It is important to identify if this is an inner-church project that will be primarily for members and friends who are already engaged in our ministry or if this is a project that will build relationships with an external audience or be a way to serve the wider community. The answers to the WHO questions impact every aspect of a new idea, from who we bring to the table to plan to how we advertise. We answer these questions in relation to other projects we are already working on, and we strive for a mix of internal and external events and projects, knowing that building relationships and building up our discipleship is as important as serving our neighbors.

This work of discernment might take ten minutes if it's a one-off project or it might be a series of meetings if it's something that requires significant investment or represents a new ministry area for us. We might reach our yes or no at any point in the process, but going through the process helps us under-

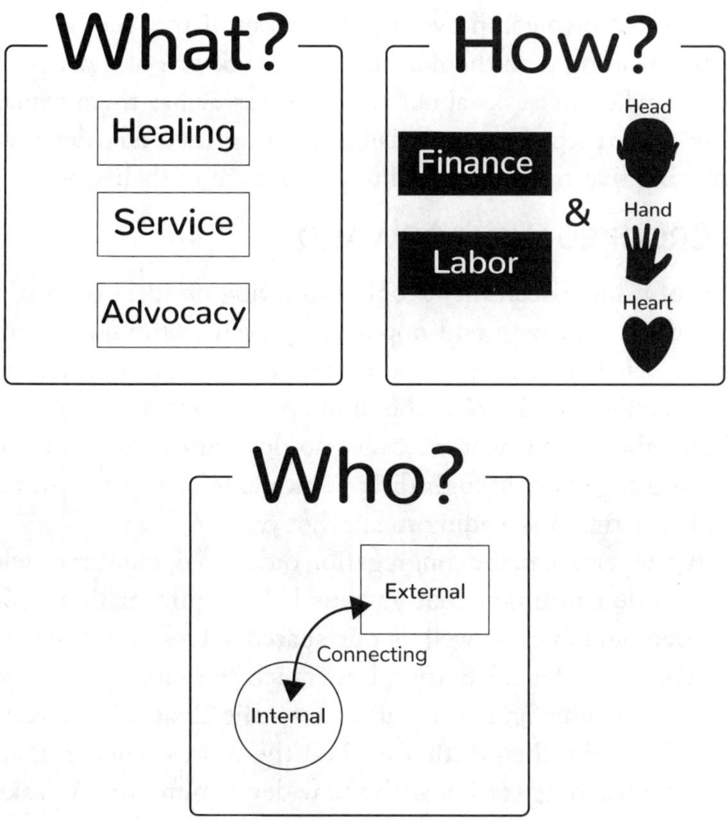

Figure 1. What? How? Who?

stand where that yes or no is coming from and feel grounded in the decision, and it helps hold our leaders accountable when the rest of the congregation starts asking questions. It may also help us discover new ideas or interests and plant seeds that lead to future endeavors.

More than anything, these discussions help our leaders leave their team meetings feeling like they have engaged with the vision of the congregation, that the discussion they had was meaningful, and that their contributions to the discussion helped shape the future of the church one way or another. It helps build ownership over our shared ministry, whether I am in the meeting with them or not. I get to be one of those pesky people who later asks about their process or has them explain how they reached their decision, trusting they dug deep and knowing that they had a tool to guide them in their work.

A CROOKED WAY FORWARD

Part of using discernment tools and trying on ideas is trusting that there is growth and opportunity even in the no's. Living into a vision isn't a linear path and could more accurately be described as a corkscrew. The difference is that when you have clarity about what you are called to do, you can keep moving forward together through disappointments or short-term no's while trusting it is leading to another yes.

A few years ago, my congregation did a sweeping survey with an outside consultant that gave us helpful information about our demographics as well as our shared values and hopes for the church. After celebrating how much the survey told us we loved our church and how primed for a Big Project we were, we picked out the themes that elicited the most excitement, and we did a listening session with the wider community. We asked community leaders with different organizations, like the local library, the head of senior services, our nearest school principals: what are the greatest needs of the population you serve? If a local nonprofit were to build a program or partner with you, what would the dream project be and what needs would that meet? Who else should we be talking to in the community? These discussions were super interesting and taught us a lot about our neighbors and surrounding neighborhoods. There were real needs in our community—like mass transit issues—that we did not feel equipped to meet. Then there were other needs that excited us and intersected with our own gifts: a need for an afterschool space for middle school and high school students at schools within a one mile radius of our church, job training opportunities for gender queer and trans young adults, and food accessibility outside of a traditional food pantry that manifested into an idea for a pay-what-you-can cafe that provided job training to LGBTQ folks. We felt we were in a healthy enough place financially that instead of envisioning a capital campaign to support generic enhancements of our building, we could raise funds to begin one of these outward facing community projects. We announced the ideas to the congregation and put out signup sheets for exploratory committees on each of the themes.

What the survey and conversations didn't account for was that even though we were healthy, wealthy, and ready for growth, we were still only two years past a lengthy and emotionally turbulent interim period in the church. We were excited for the future and ready to do something—in theory. When it came time to form exploratory committees on each of these projects to really examine what kind of energy, infrastructure, staff and volunteer support, and resources they would require, our signup sheets remained blank. A few arm twists and encouragement got some spots filled, but nowhere near the energy we would need to even explore.

This was before we created our discernment tool and even though we naturally covered most of its bases, we left out one important one: did we have the real, live, not hypothetical, people ready to lead with experience, passion, and available time? Not at that point in time. The whole congregation loved the idea of making a significant impact on our local community, but we did not have the people power to bring it to life at that moment. We were restless for growth, but we were still in the contemplation and pre-contemplation stage of change. And that was okay. Part of our vision became really shoring up and tightening what we were already doing instead of creating something extra—for now.

Did I just tell you a whole visioning process that ultimately did not succeed as planned? Yes. Were you reading this story expecting to roll your eyes at the thought of a congregation that magically started a new nonprofit and reached great heights after one congregational survey? Probably. Well, that's not us. The lesson I took is that visioning is constant work, reevaluation, and adaptability/change. We learned important things about ourselves in this process.

Part of having a vision is being able to separate "That would be great to do!" and "That would be great to do…in theory." We have to be able to admit to ourselves what we're up for and say no to the things that don't fit, even if we already started the process. Vision doesn't mean tunnel vision where you are so focused on the outcome that you ignore warning signs that say things like "road closed ahead," "turn around now," "you can't get there from here." Vision means experimenting, trying things on, saying no when it doesn't work, and finding the things that do really fit.

During the same year as our "failed" vision process, we voted to become an Environmental Justice congregation with a designated covenant, something we had dabbled in and worked on for over a decade but finally committed to as an ongoing ministry. That decision has given our Green Team roots and an invitation to expand and keep exploring new ways to engage that ministry area. That same year we also listened to how much people loved small group opportunities, so we expanded our offerings and deepened our understanding of what small group ministry might be and now more people than ever are engaging in it in one way or another.

Three years later we are still benefiting from what we learned in exploring and trying on a particular vision for our congregation to inform our newest vision process. We already knew some things about who we were and what we were willing to do, so we didn't have to start from scratch. We didn't know it at the time, but that first process was a long-term building vision for what was to come in the future. We have to have a lens that is longer than we can imagine in order to step into an unknown future together.

There are definitely times and ways a church should be nudged in a particular direction, and it is important that we have tools to help keep us moving with purpose. But we're not called to be a Church of All Things for All People. Letting go of that image will mean letting go of some of our self-importance or ideas about what a "good" church does. It also means letting go of something about the way things once were or what our passions were at another point in time in order to create a vision or goals that reflect the current congregation.

As the pastor, I might not be the person who is in charge of greenlighting new projects or crafting the vision of who we are called to be, but I am here to ask questions that get folks talking and dreaming together, that help us listen to God's presence and envision what our next great thing might be. If I spend a meeting asking questions but not offering up a single answer, I feel like it has been a good use of my time. Questions lead to deeper conversations and big dreams. These are not questions to answer alone, but are conversation starters with your leadership groups, your elders, your youth, and everyone in between. This work is the work of the whole church together—it takes us all together to craft and own the vision of the church. Here are some questions to get you started:

When was the last moment you felt the Holy Spirit at work in your church? That's church talk for: what made you really excited to be a part of your church? What were you doing? Who were you doing it with? Who was leading or who had done the planning? As amazing as it was, how would you go back and change it to make it even better?

What demographic is your church really awesome at serving? How did that develop? For instance, if you have a rockin' ministry presence for elders, has that always been the center of your congregation? What does ministry for that demographic look like? If the church stopped providing ministry to that demographic, where else would they find those same resources or community outside the church? Or would they not? How can this ministry be further strengthened?

Who are your community partners? What are the greatest needs of the populations they serve? If a local nonprofit were to build a program or partner with them, what would the dream project be and what needs would that meet? Who else do they think you should be talking to in the community?

Collaborative visioning taking the pressure off the pastor and frees our time for other aspects of ministry. By adding more voices to process, we can save our voice or use it to amplify other people's ideas and hopes for the church. It also means if the pastor steps back, whether it's for sabbatical or because other priorities have emerged, congregational leaders are equipped to continue their visioning work together. This shift helps me breathe a sigh of relief knowing that the hopes and dreams of the congregation are not mine alone to manage or manifest.

Wednesday: Committee Work Makes the Dream Work

One of my favorite parts about working and serving in the church is meetings. Whenever I publicly admit this, for some reason people always grin and pause, as if they are waiting for me to share the punchline. It starts to get awkward as it slowly dawns on them that I earnestly adore meetings and am grateful that they are a part of church life. Early on folks told me, "Just wait, you'll change your mind," but it hasn't happened. I recently looked back on my calendar last year and estimated that I attended over 1,000 meetings, a mix of committees and teams and one-on-one meetings with leaders behind the scenes. That was a conservative estimate, but big enough to say that after a decade of ministry, my love is not in danger of fading.

And.

(It's a big And.)

Meetings are terrible. A bad meeting can send you into prayer but it's more of a prayer of "WHY GOD WHY?!" I have been in meetings where people leave ninety minutes later looking like zombies instead of leaving full of passion for the church. This can happen when committees meet with no real purpose or clarity about the tasks before us. It can happen when no one wants to lead, and we end up wandering in the desert for forty years instead of planning the upcoming Advent program in forty minutes. It can happen when we don't have an awareness about the "stuff" we bring with us into a meeting—our stress, our resentments, our impatience—and it accidentally leaks all over the people on either side of us. It can happen to the best of leaders, and if you sit in enough church meetings, it has surely happened to you. Every good church leader has a memory of a painful committee meeting. If you don't, it's probably a repressed memory.

The reason meetings are both wonderful when they are fulfilling and terrible when they feel like a waste of our time is because they are important. Meetings, especially the regular gatherings of small groups responsible for different aspects of the church life and ministry, are part of the heart of communal ministry. They are part prayer and part business. They are places where we speak dreams aloud, try on new ideas, and get a pulse from the congregation. Meetings are where we learn to fight well with each other, negotiating our way through disagreements and dissent, making up, and finding our way toward a shared purpose. They are where we learn how to compromise. Where we learn how to forgive. We do this in small groups where it is safe—there is a facilitator, there is a record of what was said, there is an agenda to keep us from getting stuck in one place—with the hope that we will then be able to do this as a congregation or in informal moments that arise.

Before nurturing a laidback ministry style, I experienced weeks where it felt like all I did was prepare for meetings, attend meetings, and decompress from meetings. When meetings are not productive or meaningful, more preparation is required, they last longer than expected, and I am drained when I leave, which requires more transition time to regain my energy for the next task on my schedule. For years, I treated each committee as its own separate being. By shifting focus to building a shared culture of meetings, committees started collaborating on best practices and encouraged each other in their work. This freed up my time spent preparing for meetings and required me to attend fewer meetings because my presence was no longer critical to their success.

Laidback ministry resulted in meetings that energized instead of depleted, turning them into a springboard of creativity and excitement that positively impacted other areas of ministry. In the same way that we research and spend time crafting sermons or preparing for Bible study, it is important to craft our meeting ministries to make sure that they fulfill their purpose in the congregation and support the leaders we ask to participate in them.

During seasons when my energy is depleted and I am going through the motions, meetings can feel like déjà vu from whatever meeting I just left or had the week before, regardless of the people assembled or the goal before us. Every meeting is set by an agenda unique to that group and the task before them, but each committee's expectations about working together shapes the context for our meetings. Often these understandings are unspoken or have been reinforced through repetition over many years. When we welcome new folks onto our committees, we model through our actions and words what they can expect from the time together, and soon they are performing the same rhythms as everyone else.

These unspoken practices govern how we work, how we feel about that work, and how we support each other in the work. Change begins to happen when we speak these practices out loud and commit together to trying new ways of gathering. No matter what project is before us, we need a system or culture that helps it feel sustainable, both for the immediate tasks ahead and as we nurture lay leaders who we hope will serve on many projects to come.

Over and over, I hear committees lament and worry about how to solve problems of: getting new members on their committee, volunteer accountability and expectations (giving assignments to be done during meetings and actually completing them before the next meeting), running a meaningful meeting, finding a balance between business and building relationships, and leadership succession. These themes come up not just occasionally, but at almost every meeting in the church. Dear reader, I know you feel this in your bones. This is not a "my church" problem or a "your church" problem—church committees have struggled with these issues since the Council of Nicaea. It's past time we pull the struggle bus over on the side of the road, disembark, and look for a new vehicle to carry us. Committees and meetings themselves aren't inherently problematic, but we have to be intentional in setting them up for success.

THE HOLY GRAIL: NEW COMMITTEE MEMBERS

Committees have an asset that is unique to our organization: when a person joins a church, two of the biggest motivators are to find a sense of belonging and to find a way to be of service. Church members want to make a difference, whether it is on Sunday morning or on behalf of the church in the wider community. This is a huge gift! Part of our work is done for us because we do not need to convince people that service will positively benefit their life—they come to us looking for ways to serve.

Here is what I witness happening most often with this gift: we take that new person's energy and excitement for service and plop it into a committee. We add them to the email list and tell them the date and time of the next meeting. When they first come, we do a quick round of introductions (maybe) and then dive into the business as scheduled, picking up where we left off the month before. The new person might have questions, but they are cognizant about taking up too much space because someone has already said, "Let's make sure we're done by 8:30pm because I need to get home." Or they feel like they should be able to follow more closely because everyone else is nodding their heads and contributing at every turn. They leave that first meeting with more questions than answers, wondering if this was the right fit after all or if they bit off more than they can chew. They come to the next meeting but are more reserved. Eventually they start making excuses as to why they can't attend, and in a year the old committee is lamenting how difficult it is to recruit new members to their team.

We usher new folks directly onto a leadership team but do very little in the way of assessing their skills, orienting them to the specific work and expectations of that team, or creating an atmosphere for them to thrive. Even when we do make space in the context of a meeting, we rarely follow up between meetings for a one-on-one conversation to answer questions or share more information in an informal setting. We also rarely ask people what their experience was like joining a new committee or how the church could have better equipped them to serve.

When someone says, "Yes, I'll join a church committee" for the first time, I personally know I'm so excited by their new energy that I never think to pause long enough to ask things like:

- What is your experience serving on a volunteer committee or team?
- When you hear "group project," what feelings does that evoke?
- What kind of monthly time commitment do you have available right now?
- Are you a dreamer or a doer? A big picture planner or someone who loves diving into details?
- How do you handle compromise or disappointment?

Knowing the answers to these questions or questions like these would help myself, staff, and our key lay leaders in orienting and equipping that raw energy and excitement so that it supports the new person as well as the committee they join. Pausing long enough to ask questions helps us set reasonable expectations, opens the door for mutual conversation and learning, and lets the new folks know this is a place where questions are encouraged. It's not about gatekeeping or placing barriers to leadership. It's about making sure all parties are walking the same path and clearing out obstacles that might prevent that energy from being sustained or passed on to others.

FINDING PURPOSE

If we are so eager for new blood that we don't stop to discern or ask questions, you better believe we are also afraid of what will happen if we "allow" someone to step down from a commitment and leave us with a dreaded vacancy. We worry we will find ourselves with dwindling numbers or no one willing to serve, so we do away with term limits, or write so many term renewals into our bylaws that eventually we lose count of how long it has been (because record keeping is another common woe from our committees!) and we jokingly start folks all over again without so much as a month off. I can't think of a single commitment of mine, other than my relationship with my wife, that has lasted a whole decade, but I can name many, many church members who have spent a decade or longer serving on the same committee.

What underlies these frustrations is that every church leader I've ever talked to feels like they are alone in these predicaments. When they start to think about vacating their spot, committee chairs feel like they are letting down their team or are not living up to the legacy of the person who served for sixteen years before the mantle was unexpectedly hoisted onto them. We don't make space on our agendas for real talk about the struggles and challenges of our shared work, and even if there was time, we are afraid that if we are too honest, we'll never find a volunteer to lead again. This leaves our strongest, most capable, faithful volunteers feeling isolated, burned out, and ill-equipped.

After a season where these themes and frustrations felt particularly strong across different areas of the church, our Church Council needed to take action and called all of our committee chairs together. It took individual invitations and persuasive publicity to convince them that another evening in a meeting at the church would not just be worth their time, but would be a time of empowerment, collaboration, and support.

The agenda was loose—no handouts, no Robert's Rules, no voting. We created a space to ask questions and gave participants permission to name the challenges they were facing and maybe discover some meaning or purpose in this underappreciated world of church lay leadership. The "we" that hosted the evening was the church's council and clergy, not there to add our observations but instead to hold space, listen, and capture their reflections.

After a whole lot of cajoling, almost every committee chair and co-chair attended. When they arrived, there were Post-It charts on three tables around the room and each chairperson was invited to visit the tables and write down their responses, as much or as little came to them spontaneously. They could add check marks next to the phrases already written down that also resonated with them.

- What are the challenges your committee has?
- What are the strengths and gifts of your committee? What are you really good at?
- What support do you need as a leader in this church?

After twenty minutes of writing, we posted the sheets and read through the responses. For every written challenge, there were at least two checkmarks next to it; sometimes a few added exclamation points underscored what a big frustration it was. These were the same themes that came up in individual conversations and committee meetings: recruiting new members, leading a meeting with meaning and purpose, and encouraging committee members to serve while allowing them the grace to make an exit when it was time.

The strengths and gifts surprised us, though. There was less overlap in these notes. One committee spent time in every meeting doing a meaningful check-in with each other. One centered themselves in prayer at the beginning and end of each meeting (I know! I know! Only one?!). Another felt like they were connected to a supportive network of volunteers in the church, something other committees lamented not having. One committee took the time to create a very thorough handbook, and it transformed their institutional knowledge and how they could onboard new members. One was clear on their mission and another embraced completing assignments between meetings.

Each committee had a different strength and we spent time asking them to share the stories behind these: how did that team build a culture of sharing their personal lives before pivoting to business? Who leads the devotion and how do you address a spiritual reluctance to choose one and share? Where did those volunteers come from and how can we get some for ourselves? And do you really use that handbook? Leaders benefitted from hearing what others were doing. By talking openly, they started to feel like they weren't alone in the work.

In this gathering, committee chairs heard from our council and clergy that even with the challenges they faced, they were doing a good job and weren't letting down the church, past leaders, or their committees. Listening to these insecurities and isolation echo throughout the room made my heart ache. We perpetuated patterns of guilt and shame that were incompatible with our faith values. Instead of equipping our leaders to live into a fulfilling call to service in the church, we burned them out. This was a room full of teachers, social workers, business executives, and little league coaches—they were highly accomplished people in other aspects of their life, but at church they felt like they could never quite measure up. The problem wasn't them; it was a leadership system that did not set our leaders up for success.

On that first night, we focused on sharing stories. The stress rolled down their shoulders when people realized they were not alone in their concerns and support was available to them. Connections were made and ideas were shared. Everyone affirmed the desire to do this again and to stay in touch. It became very clear this was just the beginning. Sharing ideas and naming the concerns was a great first step, but these leaders and their committees needed more.

We didn't have the staff power to triage every committee individually—we had tried that for the last 175 years and look where we ended up. Instead, we needed to look at the information we collected that night and create supports that utilized the strengths of the different committees to teach each other and assuage their shared challenges. A member of council, a brilliant lay woman who had extensive experience creating trainings, led us in developing a series of events that all the committees would be invited to in order to streamline our ability to share information and learn together. The result was a three-part leadership development series that happened throughout the year. This series created the pivot we needed to imagine and build a new leadership and committee culture in the church.

Part One: Gather the Leaders of the Lay Leaders

We realized that a gathering of team chairs should not be a one-time thing but should happen annually. It's an opportunity for new chairs to feel like they have a support system and for older chairs to be replenished in their role. This meeting was part support group, part idea share, part opportunity for clergy and church president to get a temperature feel for where people were. This was a response to so many lay leaders saying, "I feel like I'm the only one who has this issue." In reality, everyone's usually having the same issues, and they're often basic things that need to be reinforced, like setting an agenda and circulating it beforehand, devotionals, volunteer management, and leadership retention.

This was a space of authenticity and honest truth telling. In facilitating this gathering, it was important to hold the uncertainties or challenges of the group and move them into a place of feeling supported (or not alone) and foster hope for their leadership, their ministry team, and the church. Nothing feels more demoralizing than going into a meeting that is a dumping ground for all your stress and frustrations and leaving feeling like you are covered in your own doo-doo and everyone else's as well. Picking up the collective doo-doo is not about providing instant solutions but is about helping people feel heard, creating community, and leading them toward tools to cultivate different outcomes.

Part Two: Practice Passing on Practical Information

Once we heard from the leaders of our leaders, it was time to gather with everyone—every member of a ministry team or committee and the church staff. With everyone together, we could share churchwide updates and information: mundane details like how to publicize events and big information like what the current long-term and short-term visions are and how teams can incorporate them into their ministry. This gathering equipped our committees to represent the church as a whole and gave them the tools they needed to operate in our system. Because they received this information together, they heard each other's questions and everyone left on the same page—no more silos.

Because ownership matters, my congregation's Church Council were the conveners and hosts of this gathering, rather than having the pastor or staff leading it. Every year the underlying theme for this gathering was the same: gratitude. There was a lot of information sharing, but it always came back to gratitude for the commitments that people made, the ideas they shared, and the service they did in the church.

When we had everyone in the same room, we could convey big church news or themes. This was our annual chance to make sure everyone was on the same page, but in a more intimate, interactive way than an all-church annual meeting. We heard from the moderator/president, the pastors, the office administrator. The office administrator was always the most popular speaker! I had never thought about how many people talked to our administrator on the phone or emailed with them but had no idea who they were because they only worked Monday through Friday and most of our church members come to the building on Sunday morning and in the evening. This was a time to put faces to names and ask questions that congregants might otherwise feel reluctant to reach out and ask, a time to break down assumptions and pass on well kept secrets or insider knowledge like where the supply closets were or how to get event flyers made—all really important information that helps us build the kingdom of God. This was their chance to shore up communication practices and procedures.

No topic was too trivial because the practical parts of ministry are often the parts that we forget to teach people and they tend to be different in every church or organization. We reflected on all of the recurring gripes we had during the previous year and then communicated the desired practices en masse. It relieved tension that the church had built up over time. Staff expressed how refreshing and yet strange it felt to start talking about something other than ongoing committee complaints. Can you imagine?

After the first year we did this, we created a two prong start time with new leaders invited thirty minutes prior to the general meeting, which provided an opportunity for brand new committee members to meet together, receive specific support, and be onboarded into volunteering for the church. We gave out organizational charts of the staff and committee structure, the basic things they need to know to be successful, and simple institutional knowledge that we take for granted when we've been doing it for so long. Doing this as a church rather than counting on each team to do it allowed them to focus on the particularities of their committee in their individual meetings and added a layer of support to leaders. It also created a community. Oftentimes there was only one new person per committee per year, which can feel overwhelming or isolating, but gathering them together created a cohort of new leaders and made them feel unified in their recent commitments.

Each time we started advertising these events, we got the usual lukewarm response of "oh joy, another night at church." But we persisted, kept encouraging folks, and overwhelmingly, the feedback we received after each event was incredibly positive. Never before have I heard so many folks say, "Yes, this meeting was worth my time!" Maybe that was because we didn't think of it as a meeting. We planned it as a mini-retreat that was focused on sharing information and introducing individuals to each other and to the work of the church.

During these annual all-church leadership events, I felt a mix of pride and purpose. Why did it take so long for us to bring our leaders together? Why did we settle so deeply into our separate silos that we couldn't see what could be gained by coming together? I was always surprised by how many people told me they didn't know what the other committees were or what work they did on behalf of the church. I take a lot for granted as a pastor. I've grown so used to examining the different parts of the church closely that I forget most people don't pay that much attention or don't have access to all the resources that spell it out. And when we invite people to join a committee or participate in a ministry, we only tell them about the ministry, not about all the other silos in the church that may directly or indirectly impact their ministry.

I found it helpful for this annual gathering to happen soon after the all-church annual meeting or whenever new leaders join or new committees form. We invited and encouraged committees to make this their meeting for the month instead of it being "one more thing." We talked about how the teams all fit together to form one body and likened it to our body's annual checkup.

Part Three: Relationship Building and Meaning Making

The final gathering of the year, held in the fall after the start of our program year, was more of a workshop than a retreat. It served a need we heard leaders state: they wanted to spend time together on a monthly basis in meaningful connection but often didn't know how to organize something that would facilitate this enduring contact. We invited our leaders to dive deeper into one skill or theme, doing exercises as teams, goal setting, evaluation, etc. If the retreat was focused on empowering every member of our committee to feel equipped and connected to the larger ministry and systems of the church, the fall workshop helped our committees work together, reflect on their purpose, and spend time together away from the constraints of their monthly meeting.

This evening was led by an outsider to the teams. It could be a staff member or clergy, a church member not currently serving, or someone from outside of the congregation. This is a great opportunity to invite a clergy colleague who is a skilled facilitator or offers expertise in the topic at hand. The focus was engaging, creative team building.

At one gathering, we invited each committee to work together using miscellaneous craft supplies to create a symbol for their team and demonstrate their role within the congregation. We facilitated an exercise that dove into the spirituality and business of meetings that included small group discussions about the challenges and opportunities of finding a balance between the two. We had a brief presentation on goal setting that helped the committees learn how to set goals for the program year. And all throughout, we modeled meeting best practices with opening and closing prayers, sharing an agenda (and sticking to it), making sure everyone actively participated, and honoring everyone's time by ending when we said we would end. This whole gathering took two hours. It was active, engaged multiple modes of learning, fostered relationships, and equipped committees to continue the conversations on their own. Two hours! That's less time than I take to binge my favorite television shows in one night!

Six hours a year—three evenings of two-hour sessions—created the pivot we needed to develop a more sustainable leadership culture and empower our teams to function in new ways. Focused time together was the key, as was intentionally thinking about how we wanted to communicate different kinds of information in ways that would help people remember and integrate it into their work. We used live speakers sparingly, preferring to give people time to connect with one another rather than being talked at. Other topics could be handled with short funny videos, like a ninety-second reminder on who is responsible for locking the building at night and what that procedure is. If you put me in front of a group and asked me to talk about this, I would spend five minutes on what a carefully edited video can accomplish in one minute. That extra four minutes matters when you want people to feel like they had a full, enriching, engaging evening.

When we started this leadership series, there was skepticism that it would work. To be honest, it wouldn't have been successful if not enough people participated. Part of the Holy Spirit magic was feeling like we were all there together, learning as one church leadership group. It would have broken down if we were unprepared and couldn't execute a meaningful evening or people felt like they were the only one from their team who showed up. We would have seen a radical decline in numbers four months later when we advertised the next event.

I'm not going to mislead you: planning these three evenings took a lot of work. Council talked about it two months ahead of time to clarify what the goals were. A planning team of two worked out the details and publicized the event. A month ahead of time we invited speakers, facilitators, and folks to provide hospitality and snacks. It took a lot of energy to make things appear effortless and run smoothly!

The intensive work leading up to the events was worth it because it made the rest of the year that much more productive and meaningful. I spent more time talking ministry with folks than I did holding space for their complaints and concerns. I was able to invest my time into programs and ideas rather than constant leadership development.

It takes time to shift church culture from being stuck to feeling empowered. It's worth the investment. It's worth sticking with it. It saved my ministry and reenergized our church's leadership. We were a congregation that by all accounts was thriving, but when you looked beneath the surface you could see how tired folks were. Every leader and staff person had a role to play in making this shift a success, from facilitating or speaking to showing up as an active participant. As a pastor, my role was to encourage, to name out loud the feelings we had when we were together, and to thank everyone for playing their part. I was the Energizer bunny, bringing that energy to the space when people were sapped of it, connecting people together and celebrating our shared ministry. Energizing them energized me. We all won, and ultimately it freed me up to focus on other aspects of congregational life and set down a too-heavy load.

MANY SIZES FIT ALL

I used to look for the one model that would fit all of my committees. I thought that there was surely an outline I could hand my chairperson and send them on their way. But it's more complicated than that. It requires getting to know your leaders and adapting the model to fit them. Determine what is important to each committee and know that there is more than one way to get there. Some committees thrive with timed agendas, while others need an agenda as a loose guide to be able to get lost in brainstorming or event planning. Some teams, no matter how much you coax them, will only quickly check in with each other at the beginning of the meeting. I find this is particularly true for groups over eight people, while a more intimate team, like my worship team of six people, flies through the agenda just so they have an excuse for the real conversations and check-ins to begin once the business part of the meeting is over.

Even tasks like recordkeeping and committee resources should reflect the individual cultures of our committees. There might be overall guidelines in the church, but they should be loose enough to be tailored to every committee's needs. For example, a buildings and grounds committee created a very thorough handbook. It had photos that walked people through how to do rounds of the church during lockup on Sunday morning and it explained where important mechanical parts of the church were and how they were used for those committee members who weren't mechanically inclined. Their handbook was a teaching tool, not just an historical archive, and it was actively used at every meeting. Expecting that same level of detail for a committee in charge of fellowship events might result in frustration or feel like a burden. A more valuable resource for that team is a record of the events they planned: the budget, what food was served, how many people participated, examples of past publicity, etc. They could plan new events drawing from past experience.

Groups feel empowered when they have options, and they thrive when they feel like they have permission to develop their own tools over time to meet their changing needs. Look for ways to bring the less-intuitive-but-still-essential parts to a committee. If they get anxious about who is going to lead the monthly devotional but understand the importance of starting the meeting with some spirituality (and ending it, too, if you're gonna get wild!) then create a packet of devotionals available to every team. We store ours on our online cloud so that no one has to remember to bring it, print it out, etc. Someone in each group has the app on their phone and is able to pull it up. Usually that someone is me, but I'm happy to pass my phone to the person next to me to read aloud or teach them how to download it on their phone for next time.

When committees can articulate what they need to succeed and work together to create that, it empowers their ministry and builds healthy systems of accountability. Very few people join church committees for the administrative thrill of creating systems (although those folks are out there and hallelujah for their gifts!) But maintaining a well-crafted system is much less work than struggling with something that doesn't work.

ROLE OF CLERGY

Equipping and reorienting committees is a worthwhile effort because they can (and should) be a source of energy, focused purpose, and relationship building for the congregation. I am never the person in a committee meeting to say, "I'll do that task!" Instead, I try to work with chairs to determine what the tasks are ahead of time, craft agendas, and coach them on how to find volunteers for the job at hand. An individual meeting with a committee chairperson has the potential to equip them to lead and might then allow me to not even be present at the committee meeting. It is a more focused role that nurtures an expansive committee system.

Having read about the shift to meetings with purpose and a focus on equipping lay leaders, you can begin to see why I love meetings. I love them because they aren't mine. They are led by empowered leaders and are a vehicle the church has to make good ministry happen. I love meetings and committees because I see them as an integral part of our leadership development and part of a cycle that has to happen every year. It's not a one-and-done workshop or a retreat, but an ongoing practice where there is always going to be a mix of seasoned and new leaders together. When I am in a meeting, I am there to listen, to affirm, to support—hoping that everyone will come away with the same love I have, or at least say, "That was a meeting that was worth my time."

Thursday: Collaboration

Once upon a time, there was a small New England suburb that was home to three churches from the same denomination. Their gleaming white meetinghouses sat at each of the town borders, forming a triangle that encompassed the whole community. Although they are fully autonomous congregations today, the three began as one, established along with the town in 1692.

The story goes that as the town expanded in the booming era of the 1700s, people found it inconvenient to give up half of their Sunday to travel the five miles by foot or horseback to attend worship. The farmers especially complained about having to sacrifice time in their fields to sit in pews alongside the city folk downtown. The church soon yoked two new churches, forming a sisterhood of congregations united in theology and polity across the geographical distances.

Three-hundred years later, the family vehicles upgraded from horse-drawn buggies to minivans. The five miles shrank from a half day of travel to twelve minutes roundtrip, but the proverbial distance remained. The three sister churches found other ways to differentiate themselves. One is a close-knit family church. One has a youth group so big it represents a third of the overall membership. One still stands tall and proud as the largest and most prominent church in town. But mostly, they have 300 years of practice doing their own thing in their separate corners.

Compared to the other dozen congregations that now exist in town, the original three remain more similar than different. They share the same core values and the same liturgy. Unlike many of their neighbors, all have long embraced an explicit affirmation of LGBTQ+ folks. These churches are so similar that their members can move between congregations and feel right at home. In fact, some of their members do quietly move between the three, formally and informally, depending on their season of life.

I was once one of six clergy serving among these three sister congregations. Before I arrived, I was overjoyed with the prospect of sharing ministry with close colleagues nearby. I grew up across the country where you had to drive an hour before you encountered another church in our denomination. I was used to my small progressive church feeling like an outsider in a sea of evangelical mega-churches that set the tone for local culture and politics. I was thrilled by the opportunity these three churches had to build partnerships and do ministry in a way that impacted not just what happened inside the walls of their meetinghouses, but throughout the whole community. With so much in common, surely there would be a shared calling between our congregations, a binding together as one denominational identity. Surely we would lean on each other for support and encouragement, knowing the particular expectations and hopes placed on us as clergy could only be understood by this unique cohort of neighbors. I imagined I was joining the knights of the round table, or rather, the clergy of the shared communion table.

I slowly realized that this fairytale ministry setting had a dragon of individualism lurking nearby, breathing a wall of fire whenever we clergy or our churches imagined collaborating. We saw each other at denominational gatherings across the state and the town's annual interfaith service, but that was the extent of our collegiality. After seven years, I didn't know my sister colleagues as well as I knew the Episcopal priest or the Baptist pastor. The six of us were more likely to share our average worship attendance or news of a staffing transition than we were to share our hopes and dreams as clergy, the gifts and challenges of our congregations.

There was no animosity between the clergy, but a culture of distant politeness acted as a barrier to the vulnerability required to nurture authentic relationships. And, rather than leveraging the things we had in common to understand our unique identities, it felt like if we acknowledged the connections our congregations had, people might start to question the need to have these three separate churches.

No one spoke these dynamics out loud, but when each of us was the new clergy person in town, we inherited a 300-year-old expectation of independence before interdependence and quickly shifted our energy exclusively to pastoring our own people in our own corner of town. Soon after I arrived, I was so focused on making sure my church was The Best Church that my early daydreams of collaboration and shared purpose felt naive. How would I have the time to collaborate when I was so busy trying to build, nurture, and replicate every ministry under the sun?

I often wondered what might happen if we worked together instead of ignoring (at best) or competing (at our pettiest) with each other. What if we stopped comparing ourselves as if we were businesses fighting for customers, but started thinking of ourselves the way a school district does—collaborating across campuses to share resources, learn from one another, and support each other's leadership? What if we enthusiastically celebrated the work each congregation did knowing we were each one part in the body of Christ that needed us all to fulfill our unique purpose? What if we leaned into our shared denominational identity and built a joint legacy as part of the foundation of the town both in its origins and today?

This work requires us to move from a scarcity model (my church needs to be more, do more, grow more…) to a model of abundance. Thank God someone else is called to do that; I can more deeply focus on this other piece. Thank God for my neighbors; they are an important part of the story of how God is working in our community. Thank God I don't have to do it all myself; our community is richer for the connections and relationships our churches nurture across the body of Christ. Thank God that together we can accomplish feats that we never would have been able to do on our own.

How do we slay the dragon of individualism and competition? How do congregations come together to realize they don't need to be the hero, but that it is more swoon-worthy to admit we need each other?

COLLABORATION STARTS SMALL

Partnering with other congregations takes a strong commitment and intentionality to begin. If you thought it was draining to coordinate schedules for a meeting in one church, imagine coordinating schedules across churches with competing nights of choir practices and different meeting cultures. It is made easier when you start small, such as a project that has a clear beginning and end and won't take a year to pull off. It's even easier if it's something your congregation is already committed to but that would be enhanced with more people at the planning table.

Today I'm serving in a different town that has fewer denominational sister churches but does have a strong cohort of interfaith congregations. My church was the first of these congregations to join with our wider LGBTQ+ community in its annual Pride parade and festival. It is a defining commitment of our congregation and an outreach that draws in many of our newer members, including myself. We've been at it for over twenty years now. And you know what? We're exhausted.

The same crew of people have been building the parade float, recruiting volunteers, and staffing the table for most of those twenty years. We're a small enough church that eventually everyone feels like they have over-served their time but no one else is jumping up to take over. We have internalized a message that if we don't show up as the loudest and proudest church, we aren't doing enough to love our LGBTQ+ siblings so taking a year off is not a popular option.

Twenty years ago, we were the only church at Pride, but in the last few years we have had others join us and more want to come each year. While my people are exhausted, these congregations have all the energy and excitement of someone just starting, with a long line of volunteers, plenty of budget allotted, and more ideas than anyone can possibly implement in a year.

Last year, faced with another round of cajoling volunteers to staff the Pride booth, I spontaneously asked at an interfaith clergy meeting, "Anyone want to join my church for Pride? We have a lot of experience but we're tired." Pastors started sliding me notes with their phone numbers and messages saying, "Pick me! Pick me!" By the end of the week, we scheduled a planning meeting with representatives from five congregations.

Our combined booth at the festival celebrated the diversity of the faith community. With a range from Episcopalian to Unitarian Universalist, we created a joint flyer that pointed folks to different congregations based on their beliefs or longings. Instead of twelve volunteers for the festival (preparing swag, organizing the parade participants, staffing the booth), each church only needed three people, making it accessible to every congregation regardless of their size. Sharing fees, printing, and swag costs made it a nominal expense for each church.

Previous Pride years were successful in their own right, but at a time when we were tired and needed to shake things up, this collaboration helped us redefine what success might look like moving forward. The experienced congregations were able to offer their wisdom like, "Don't choose a spot that is downwind from the food trucks," and they could guide the other congregations through the process of what to expect, offer set-up supplies, and be steady leaders on the big day. The new congregations brought zealous energy and reminded the rest of us why we were doing this. They asked good questions, introduced fresh ideas, and helped our tent go from one you might not notice to one where people gravitated all day long. Some of that newbie energy rubbed off on my seasoned volunteers and by the end of the day we were all tired but satisfied, even joyful, at what we had accomplished together.

Finding collaborative partners can be as easy as observing what congregations around you (or that you can connect with online) are up to and asking, "Can my church join you?" It might be as small as advertising another congregation's lecture series and inviting your church folks to carpool together. Attending an event together requires minimal planning energy and is an opportunity for folks to talk about what they liked and what they have in common with that congregation. As a result, it can help them to begin seeing each other as congregations in dialogue. Other opportunities can open up by inviting another congregation to join you in something you might have done alone: movie and discussion, book group, field trip to a local museum, marching together in a parade. What are the events that would be amplified by having more people or sharing resources across congregations? What are the traditions your congregation holds to tightly but could use new folks to help reimagine or reenergize?

QUID PRO PASTOR

Moving toward collaboration requires making time to get to know your colleagues. That means making time to attend those interfaith or community clergy gatherings, reaching out to new colleagues in the months after they start a new position, and prioritizing the building of relationships as part of your ministry.

I love getting to know other pastors. This is partially because they are the closest thing I have to a coworker—they just happen to work in a different part of town. I also love getting to know what they are good at and what they are passionate about in ministry. More often than not, it's different than what I love. And more often than not, it's a skill or passion my congregation would benefit from. Instead of lamenting that I'm not more well-rounded or worrying that my congregation will find out there is someone nearby who is better at teaching Christian history than I am, I invite them to come teach a series at my church. Why should I do a lackluster job at something when there is someone in my area who does it better? I want to put my energy towards the things I excel at while still allowing my congregation to have experiences they are craving or that will better equip them to be disciples.

Sometimes I wonder if Jesus kept a group of leaders around him not because he couldn't do it all himself, but because he knew he needed to focus on parts that were specifically his responsibility and ask others to do the rest. While he was healing people in the house, someone was outside telling the crowds the backstory of who Jesus was and about his relationship with

God. While he was walking on water and calming storms, someone else was reading the navigation map and another was steering the ship. That band of leaders worked together to minister to people, pooling their talents and skills to minister to a larger group than any of them—even Jesus—could have managed on their own.

I imagine the disciples had different skills and preferences. Some gravitated toward the elders in the crowd while others got the youth organized; some were great with groups while others shined one-on-one. We most often understand the disciples from their gaze toward Jesus, but they were also a cohort of collaborators, confidants, and colleagues that had to navigate ministry in partnership with one another. What parts of their shared ministry left them fulfilled? What did they feel like their growing edges were? How did they lean on each other and support one another so that two or three or twelve of them together could fill the shoes Jesus left behind?

We might not have a detailed view of how the first disciples navigated ministry together, but Paul's letters to the early Christian church spend a great deal of time talking about collaboration and how to navigate the variety of needs, egos, and needy egos between church leaders. His description of the gifts of the spirit in 1 Corinthians begins with a reminder that "there are different kinds of service but the same God." No gift brings someone closer to God than other people. The point is to know what your gift is, use it, and hold space for other people's spiritual gifts to be utilized as well.

One Lent, a colleague and I collaborated on a swap that enabled us to use each other's gifts in service to our separate congregations. I had people longing for contemplative spiritual practices and I'm rubbish at that stuff. Put me in a labyrinth and I just start doing a David Bowie impression and singing, "You remind me of the babe! The babe with the power!" As it turns out, the Methodist minister in the next town over is a natural contemplative and leads a weekly class for her folks. Her people were longing for racial justice classes, which just happens to be in my wheelhouse.

We agreed that Lent would be more meaningful for our churches and us if we could all focus on our passions, so we arranged a swap. Our congregations were thrilled with the novelty of a new voice, and we didn't have to awkwardly stumble through topics we weren't equipped to lead. A huge weight rolled off my shoulders when Lent arrived. Because we focused on each of our skill sets, neither one of us was taking on more work than we could handle. We actually had a lighter Lenten load because we weren't having to spend hours researching and preparing before teaching; we could practically teach our classes in our sleep. That left a Lent season with space for my own prayer practice and spiritual development where ordinarily I would be too frazzled researching and learning to focus on my own needs.

It seems like everyone is an expert on *something* these days. As you get to know colleagues, pay attention to what they are passionate about. What part of ministry makes their eyes light up? What topic are they always going on about or encouraging you to join them on a continuing education experience for? A particularly organized group of clergy might even create their own "gifts and talents survey" that they are always making their church members fill out for themselves—a way of documenting and sharing what experiences, skills, and teaching interests they have that might be useful to neighboring congregations. File these passions away, because when it comes time to plan programs and someone asks you to lead a Lenten series on different prayer practices, you will be able to say, "That's not my expertise, but I know just who we can invite to lead it!"

COLLABORATION EXPANDS DREAMS

There are times when the ideas my congregation has are too big to be pulled off with a colleague swap, or the expert we want to invite in requires more funds than our budget allows. The approach I use is to seek out congregations or organizations that might be interested in partnering to bring someone in, and then split the costs. One of the greatest joys in ministry is finding other people to help pay for our wild ideas and bring them to life. It's easier to try on new ideas or to think outside the box if we have relationships in our wider community that we might be able to tap into to make those dreams become a reality. Again, this requires getting to know your neighbors and finding out who might be on a similar journey as your people.

A year ago, my congregation fell in love with a workshop leader who charges $5,000 plus travel expenses at a minimum for a one-day workshop. They are a phenomenal, nationally known speaker and facilitator, but because they happened to live only an hour away from our church, we felt like the travel expenses would be a bargain. But let's be real: $5,000 is our workshop budget for ten years, so in order to imagine hosting this workshop, we had to first imagine who we might invite to host with us. We called our Episcopal neighbors who we knew were passionate about the same topic. They got excited and found some money in their budget. They then called their diocese who had a working group interested and found some budget money in order to send some people to participate. We reached out to a local community organizing group who we knew were dealing with these same issues and extended an invitation—they were also on board. With four groups of varying sizes and budget constraints working together, we not only met our $5,000 budget, but were able to provide lunch for all the participants.

Our congregation averages thirty to forty people for special workshops, and fifty to seventy people if we are *really* excited about the topic. Bringing in another congregation doubles the headcount, which can make people feel like they are a part of something truly special. Numbers shouldn't matter, but they do.

There are important reasons to hold small group experiences and important reasons to have large group opportunities. We need a diversity of experiences to accommodate different learning styles and create multiple paths to deeper discipleship. Being a smaller congregation (and vice versa) doesn't mean you are limited in the types of engagement or experiences you can offer; it just means you need community partners.

There was once a time when someone would share an idea that sounded amazing but was too big of an undertaking for our congregation and I used to think, "That's a great idea but it can't ever happen." Now my response is, "That's a great idea. Who are the partners that can make this happen?" I love to encourage our teams and leaders to come up with the biggest idea imaginable, something that seems ridiculously inspiring but also out of reach. We can always scale back, but when we lead with our heart's dreams and have a network of partners in place, those out-of-reach ideas start to feel a little more possible. Not everything has to be big, but not everything has to be limited by the resources at hand in an individual congregation.

In the process, we had reached out to other congregations as well who ended up passing on the opportunity for one reason or another, but that was okay. Taking the risk by making the ask is part of the process; those conversations became the beginnings of future collaborations on other topics. The hardest part is making an ask. You might hear a few no's, but even then simply asking might plant a seed for the future. My sensitive ego worries that if I propose an extravagant idea or make a big ask, my colleagues will think I am overly extravagant or perhaps not a good steward. Instead, they hear permission to voice their own extravagant ideas.

If inviting colleagues into dreaming big with you feels vulnerable, who are the trusted close colleagues you can start by asking? Or are there folks you can describe the dream to without adding an ask? Talking about it widely not only multiplies the chances of others joining you (and bringing their coffers and their people with them) but also gives you the opportunity to fine tune the dream as you keep revisiting it. Ask yourself: what is holding us back from dreaming big? What are the barriers to inviting other churches to dream with us or join our dream?

LEAVE YOUR EGO AT THE DOOR

Growing into a mindset where the church down the street feels like a collaborator instead of competition takes practice. It requires rejecting the idea that every congregation is competing for the same pot of people. When I start thinking of church in terms of who has the biggest membership roll or the flashiest vacation Bible school theme, I lose sight of the fact that each of us has something unique to offer. That reframe starts by remembering that my congregation has a particular vision and identity that is unique to us—we aren't the off-brand version of the big church down the street. We are our own brand of quirky, Jesus-loving, charming characters who are faithfully attracting a niche group and helping them be the most faithful people they can possibly be. Embracing our own singularity also requires adopting a "more is more" belief that we actually want more churches to help share in the ministry across the community. When congregations start to do the work of justice, they quickly realize that it's not just about changing hearts, it's about changing massive systems and institutions that impact people's lives. We need as many co-conspirators as possible to make changes or breakdown these entrenched systems. That requires partnerships with bold neighbors who aren't afraid of good trouble.

Even so, when a church starts to look a little too similar to my own, it's a real effort to leave my ego at the door and see past our surface-level similarities to embrace them. A few years ago, a new church formed in town. And because we shared a denomination and core values, I had major jealousy vibes in the beginning. I was part of the older, established church in town and just two miles away there was a new worship space so cool that millennials were the church elders. I have always felt like my current congregation was doing a distinct thing in our community, especially in regard to LGBTQ+ affirming ministries, but this new church was so LGBTQ+ they dropped the acronyms and jumped right to queer. My folks were excited to have a new resource in the community but also a little anxious that we would lose one of our core public identities to the new kid on the block, as if there is only room for one queer-centered religious space in our city.

The reality is that the LGBTQ+ community is as diverse as any other community with many different needs. Before the new church opened, I would have LGBTQ+ folks in the community talk to me and tell me that although they love our congregation and their warm welcome, it still feels too much like a traditional church for them to be comfortable coming inside on Sunday morning. I get that. And now when I have that conversation I can say, "Have you heard about the new place? It sounds like it might be a perfect fit for you, and worship isn't even on Sunday morning." What a relief to be able to encourage them to try a place that is a better fit instead of having a semi-miserable person sitting in the back of the congregation each Sunday morning thinking, "I guess this is better than nothing." I want people in our pews who are excited to be there and fulfilled in our church, and I want to help them find the right fit if we can't provide that ministry.

The same is true for the new church. When young adults come in their doors and talk about missing the connection to older family members or miss being part of a big faith community, our church is their number one recommendation. We have enough to go around as long as we can make sure people are coming into the right doors. We won't know what's right for them if we don't talk and share ideas, or don't see ourselves as one wider church serving the same community.

When we take on a "more is more" attitude, we get specific and deep about the ways we are equipped to serve. We can celebrate when others do the same with their own ministries. By having multiple spaces in our community that were queer-centered, we were better serving the diversity of our community and making a bolder statement about what kind of faith culture we had in our area, without having to work twice as hard or failing all of our LGBTQ+ generations by being too generic.

I've never met a clergy person or congregation that doesn't have a rival. Sometimes it's the church down the street; sometimes it's the colleague across the country that serves a congregation suspiciously similar to yours. Some of my church members even have rival churches—perhaps a sibling's church or the church they grew up in—and they return from annual visits at their rival church with a full report for us about what they are doing (that of course we should also be doing) and what they aren't doing (that coincidentally looks like what we do well). It usually includes a lament about the dozens of young families *that other congregation* seems to attract. Who does this inner competition serve? How might we transform our rivalries—the spoken and unspoken ones—into gratitude about the strength of the wider church or gratitude that we are not alone in this ministry to live out Christ's Gospel in a challenging era? How might we see similar congregations in our town as an opportunity for collaboration, a celebration of the church universal, or an indicator of the depth of needs in our community?

Sometimes we sing "this little light of mine, I'm gonna let it shine" with enthusiasm but forget its sister verse "that little light is theirs, I'm gonna keep them in my prayers." Okay, I just made that up, but maybe we need more songs celebrating our neighbors and all the ways that they shine. When our communities have more options, more ministries, more partnerships, our congregations are able to focus on being the most authentic versions of themselves.

NURTURING COLLABORATION

When doing the work of nurturing collaboration, follow the same timeline you might with someone who visits your church the first time: get to know them, allow them to get to know you. Extend an invitation to something easy or enjoyable. For instance, we always invite new members to faith enrichment or fellowship events before asking them to join the finance committee, and we continue looking for signs this is a good match. When a new person comes to the church, it is tempting to oversell who you are in an effort to "win" their membership, but the most success comes when we are authentic—the same is true when building collegial and collaborative relationships. Not everyone is going to be your bff or your muse or your co-conspirator. Take the time to lay foundations with multiple people and organizations and see where time leads you. Remember that relationships are not linear, so what may not be a good collaboration one year or for a particular project may be a wonderful collaboration down the road.

It takes significant time to find those people who will become colleague collaborators and ministry partners, and because of the evolving nature of ministry, that work is never done. I say this for myself as much as for any reader. I have the patience of a lightning bolt and after one lunch with the new pastor in town I am plotting out the projects we'll work on together and how our congregations are going to be new best friends, only to never hear from them again because it turns out they had different priorities and dreams for community ministry. Sigh. I've learned to slow down and watch for natural opportunities to work together instead of trying to force an instant alliance. There is not a magic formula for identifying who your close colleagues and ministry partners are going to be. You want to make sure you have similar values, that they will show up when they say they are going to show up, and that you are really compatible, not just with each other, but with each other's congregations.

Collegial relationships are like every other kind of relationship, whether it is platonic, romantic, or familial: some are never going to happen, some are great for a season, some last for many years, and they all take work to nurture and maintain. Collaboration plays a big part in lightening my workload. A significant part of that is building and maintaining relationships. It takes consistent work to establish trust and mutuality, to get to know the other ministries in your community and how they do and don't align with your congregation.

I am invested in my community, not just my congregation, and that means it is to my benefit to have multiple places for people to land when they are searching for a spiritual home so that I don't have to try to make my church be all things to all people and end up disappointing everyone when we turn into the lowest common denominator. It is worthwhile to invest in the health and growth of my neighborhood congregations and their clergy to ensure we have a robust network of congregations who have overlapping values and a shared vision for our town or city. There was a time when I would have looked warily at my neighbors and only seen what I was missing in my own ministry, but today I celebrate their presence and give thanks that the more they step up, the more I can step back or step into the parts of ministry that I am most called to.

Friday: Letting Go

If I could have an answer to just one of the many great mysteries of congregational ministry, it would be: When the heck did we start settling for a one day weekend? Is this the fault of the over-abundant work ethic of a religious ancestor? Did one of Martin Luther's ninety-five theses that he nailed to the church door tell clergy they need to work while everyone else spends two carefree days on their pontoon boats? The church is infamous for being slow to change but the workforce revolution was 100 years ago. There is a deep cultural understanding that two days a week away from work is ideal for people to do their errands, mow their lawn, play board games with their kids, and meet their friends for brunch. When Ford Motor Company started instituting two-day weekends for its workforce and the idea swept the country, why did clergy not follow suit? What "suffering is good for the soul" second-rate martyr started creeping into the office on Saturday mornings to "get ahead" and ruin it for the rest of us?

Even as overworking became newly en vogue in the last decade due to the popularity of cell phones, home internet, and the eighty-hour work week as a status marker, that was nothing new for clergy. We are leaders in putting the office over family, taking work with us on vacation, and then leaving that vacation early for an unexpected church emergency.

To be fair, the first day of the work week for clergy is Sunday, and every Sunday begins with a major presentation first thing in the morning to the whole company. At least, that's how I explain it to my non-church friends when they scrunch up their faces after I tell them I can't hang out past eight o'clock on a Saturday night. We carry the weight of Sunday with us into our weekends—wanting to be the best pastor possible, feeling like the congregation is counting on us for wisdom and care, worrying about what unknown crisis waits for us in the week ahead.

Sometimes it is easier to stay in work mode than unplug and unwind for one, let alone two days. We might miss something. We didn't get our work done. That perfect sermon inspiration hasn't shown up yet. How many pastors do you know that proclaim the Holy Spirit does her best sermonizing on Saturday night? Is that really the Holy Spirit or is that the spirit of procrastination and looming deadlines? Are you sure the Holy Spirit isn't the one nudging you down from the office into bed early so you can be fresh on Sunday morning?

When I entered the workforce as a teenager, slinging shaved ice at the local Sno Shack, I fully expected to work every weekend. It was spelled out in my job contract, which was helpful because even in the summer my weekdays were reserved for band camp and one-dollar movies at the air-conditioned cinemaplex. I harbored the hope that staying in school would eventually mean landing a job that allowed me to reclaim my weekend for myself, even if it had fewer snow cone benefits. Woe is me for heeding a call to ministry and accepting that the boundaries between "work" and "rest" would become quite blurry.

I didn't learn my overworking ways from scripture, but they did come from stories. Internship supervisors and pastors-turned-seminary professors told impressionable young seminarians war stories about late nights at the office and days off working while their family did something fun without them. They came from driving by the church at odd hours and noticing my pastor's car always seemed to be there. They came from mentors and colleagues who told braggadocious stories about how it had been six, seven, eight weeks since they had a full day off. It didn't take long before I was showing off my own wounds in the form of bags under my eyes and telling my own overworked war stories.

I'm as guilty as the next pastor of idolizing working through the weekends. It's the toughest habit to break and I am just one email away from sliding back into working on my time off. There is always something else to do. There is always something vying for my attention. There is always a sermon to procrastinate writing and drag around in my mind during my days off. I'm not perfect at taking my two days a week off, but I have changed the story that I tell myself, and my behaviors follow the story: I regularly take two days off a week, usually two days off in a row. There are times when this is not the case, but that is the exception. I work hard to balance my week so that I can leave for the weekend with integrity.

MAKE LIKE ELSA AND LET IT GO

In order to live out a story that includes regular time off each week, I have to let go of:

1. The idea that I will meet all my external deadlines and internal expectations every week. I start letting go of this idea early in the week, as early as possible. I set and reset my expectations each day and try to be real with myself about what is and isn't getting done. I ask for extensions when I need them. I ask for forgiveness when I need it and I freely give it to others, be it staff or volunteers, who are also trying to balance church service with home life. I also do my best to prioritize and place tasks into flexible and inflexible categories. I know I'm capable of making and meeting necessary deadlines because after a decade of preaching, I've yet to step into the pulpit unprepared. This lets me know that if it is critical, I can and will get it done during work hours or the work week.
2. The idea that I need to be everywhere or that I am the only person who can do something. Ministry is a team sport. If it starts to feel like everything hinges on my presence or my contribution, I need to check in with the rest of the team and rebalance the equation. Either I need to pass off some pieces to other people, or we need to collectively let go of some pieces if there is no one else to take them on.
3. The idea that the project/email/phone call/deadline before me is the most important thing. Yesterday something else was the most important thing. Tomorrow it will be another most important thing. It is a seamless handoff from one urgent matter to the next, and we are the only ones with the power to pause and

> say, "This important thing can wait because my rest is also the most important thing." This means creating a mindset where rest and time away from church is a priority. Not once a year for a week's vacation or every five years for a sabbatical kind of priority, but an every single week, almost as if God commanded us to rest every seven days, kind of priority.

Taking time off means reorienting my idea of my calling to include a call to rest. Whew. Even writing that feels challenging. It feels similar to the way we focus on the commandment to love the neighbor and God but forget the part where it says to love ourselves. We are called to self: to nurture ourselves, to cultivate joy for ourselves, to create rest and renewal for ourselves. That is truly work no one else can do for us, and paradoxically, when I don't do it, I start to resent the people around me for not "allowing" me to do it or not creating space for me to do it. Nope. It is my responsibility to prioritize and create time for rest.

This reorientation is a daily practice that impacts countless little ways you approach ministry, from what you take into consideration before saying yes, to how far out you schedule meetings. There are also some concrete practices that impact bigger pieces of ministry. They helped me "find" more time in my week, thus making weekends feel more accessible. These are some of the big shifts I made that helped transform my whole year. They might be mappable onto your own experience or might allow you to brainstorm or imagine what shifts are possible in your own ministry setting. Regardless, shifting takes intentionality and, like every other aspect of laidback ministry, practice without the expectation of perfection.

WIDER CHURCH OBLIGATIONS

One of the invisible pieces of being a pastor that takes a significant amount of time is that you don't just work for and with your local church, but you also work for and with the wider church. This is true across every mainline denomination, and sometimes my wider church obligations can make me start to see the joy in being nondenominational. For some clergy, participating in the wider church can mean meetings and obligations across town or an hour away. For others their region might be so spread out that throughout the year they have to drive (or fly in the case of Hawaii!) to meetings that are several hours away, requiring an overnight stay to fully participate. The advent of the Zoom era has been a slight reprieve, taking out the long commute and enabling participation from home.

This "extra" work is not often counted in the life of the local church, and most church members don't realize how often events and meetings happen in the wider church that clergy are expected to attend. Because wider church commitments have to work around already packed congregational schedules, and want to be inclusive of lay leaders, they often happen on the weekend. That means clergy are spending their weekdays at their local church and then instead of logging off for their weekend, they are logging on to wider church Zoom calls and conferences.

Often clergy are the thread that binds their denomination to the local church. This might mean representing the church at clergy gatherings, continuing education events, or regional meetings. It can mean serving on denominational committees where you are never just Bob Potter, you are Reverend Bob Potter from Hopeside Church. Back at home in the church, it means keeping the congregation informed about decisions that are made in the wider church, connecting them with resources, and making sure they maintain a healthy denominational identity. It's the aspect of being clergy where we become part spokesperson, part salesperson, and part PR expert. And it can take a whole lot of our time.

In a recent six-week period I had on my calendar:

- A two-day clergy wellness retreat hosted by my regional conference.
- A two-day annual regional conference meeting that fell on my typical days off.
- A half-day continuing education event sponsored by the conference that I agreed to host in my church building.
- A one-day annual regional meeting (you know—because the smaller regions within the larger region need to have their own meetings).

This did not include the committee and subcommittee I serve on in our region that each meet monthly.

When I turned my calendar to a new month and saw all these things, I did an internet search for "which Christian denomination has the fewest gatherings" and investigated transferring my ordination standing. It took many deep breaths and several minutes pacing my office before I could admit to myself that even though each of these events were all important in one way or the other, there was no way I could attend them all and still have energy for my church, or prioritize rest, let alone see my wife in any meaningful way that month.

After a lot of discernment and private pep talks that I was not failing my local church, the wider Church, or God by not fulfilling all of these obligations, I made some hard decisions. I would attend the clergy wellness retreat because my level of stress over making these decisions said I needed something restorative in my month. I would go to the continuing education event because my church was the host site, so I needed to be there anyways. I decided to skip the two annual meetings and made a note in next year's calendar to commit to attending those—a decision which would surely mean saying no to something else in the future.

Even though I made decisions that still kept me involved and present in the wider church, I felt *so much guilt* for missing the two meetings. Surely, I'm not the only pastor who hears the word "annual meeting" and interprets it as "*you better go every year.*" But when I stopped looking at those meetings on their own and placed them alongside all of the opportunities I had to deepen relationships with colleagues and represent my congregation, it didn't seem treasonous to take a year off from those two meetings.

My guilt returned on the morning of the first annual meeting when I received a message from a church member letting me know they were at the meeting and should they save me a seat? Uh oh. I hadn't factored my congregation's expectations into the equation when I decided which events to bow out of. Now I felt like I was letting down the wider church AND my beloved church members. How is a pastor ever supposed to balance this impossible equation without feeling like they are worn down?!

Once I stopped feeding my anxiety dragon, you know what I realized? The most important part of the regional annual meetings is to have leadership from as many congregations as possible. Both of those annual meetings had lay representatives from my church. *It didn't have to be me.* And even better, both of the meetings had multiple reps from my church so I could stop feeling guilty about "abandoning" my church member. I wrote a quick text that explained that while I was sad not to be with them that day, they should keep an eye out for both their fellow church member and members from the UCC church down the road—a great opportunity to build relationships. The next day, when I saw the church member after worship, I thanked them for attending, asked how it went, and made a coffee date to talk about all they learned so they could pass on relevant resources to me. It turns out they weren't messaging me because they were angry that I wasn't there—they were simply trying to be polite. They had as great a time as anyone has ever had at an all-day meeting and did not harbor any resentment about my absence.

I could have helped that church member—and my perpetually guilty conscience—by making my decision earlier and communicating to my church representatives that I would not be joining them. We could have even had the congregation bless them or pray for them in worship the week before so that they would feel how important their invisible ministry was to the congregation, and the congregation could have another opportunity to see lay leadership modeled. Both of these small things would have relieved the big pile of guilt that I felt and relieved me of feeling like I needed to attend each and every meeting. Both would have happened had I followed my own advice and looked ahead in my calendar.

I reoriented myself from believing I was the only one carrying the weight of the denominational connections and began to see this responsibility, like everything else, as a shared ministry. This shift caused me to see that supporting others in their participation is as important, and sometimes more important, than my own direct participation. This allows for flexibility in organizing our local church representation, faithfulness in fulfilling our covenantal obligations in the wider church, and dexterity in balancing these things with the rest of our ministry.

HOW TO PREACH WITHOUT A SERMON

Last year I broke one of my cardinal rules: Thou shall not preach the day after returning from vacation. There are a million excuses why this was inevitable. I scheduled a vacation to visit family in California and when we tried to balance ridiculous flight prices with my wife's work schedule, my work schedule, and my family's schedule, the intersection of those competing needs meant that we arrived home on a Saturday morning after a red-eye flight. I was scheduled to preach twenty-seven hours later.

One of my other cardinal rules is that I don't write sermons while away on vacation. I don't travel with my computer. I've been trying to even leave the iPad at home, knowing that it is a slippery slope before I start reading commentaries on my Kindle app and taking notes to be transcribed into a sermon once I arrive home. I upheld the no sermonizing on vacation rule, which meant my vacation ended at eight o'clock on Saturday morning when we arrived home. My wife went to bed to make up for the lost night of sleep from the flight, and I went to sit in front of a blank screen on my laptop "just to get ideas flowing." Thirty-five Facebook posts were liked and fifty-seven spam emails deleted. One hour later, the Holy Spirit was still on vacation, and I felt demoralized. And tired. I was resentful of the looming work, but I was also resentful of the time away—this wouldn't have happened if I hadn't taken vacation.

After succumbing to a long nap, I did come back and squeak out a sermon. I could stand behind what I preached the next morning, but just barely. I had low energy and felt like I was stumbling over my words instead of passionately professing the Gospel. A part of me kept trying to reclaim the hours I put into work on Saturday—an hour here, a few minutes there, and unlike a complete day away, this slowed everything down and made me feel out of sync with my best and most integrity filled self. It also devalued worship. I counted down the minutes to the benediction when I could return home to claim the hours of downtime that I had lost the day before.

There was a fair amount of self-flagellation that took place that week after vacation. When I told my spiritual coach about my guilt in the hope that she would take pity and assure me this kind of conflict was inevitable, she said, "So what are you going to do about it?" Okay, rude. Obviously, I was a victim of impossible circumstances and couldn't be expected to change.

She rejected that idea and again asked me, "What are you going to do?" After a lot of stuttering and avoiding eye contact, I decided that transitions were as important as time away, and that every vacation going forward would include an appropriate amount of transition time, including transitioning back to preaching even if I was leading the rest of worship the next day. I also made a commitment to plan my vacations as I planned the worship calendar so that I could build in those preaching breaks with my time away.

Now I make travel arrangements so that if I am working Sunday morning, I am home by Friday night. I need that day for transition at home—settling back in, laundry, recovering from vacation. While it might feel like I am losing a coveted day away, I am ultimately gaining a greater sense of rest by taking a longer transition time. Having Saturday to fully rest makes a significant difference in my energy and focus levels. It isn't that I can't lead post-vacation, it's just that in order to honor the boundaries that keep me accountable to myself, my family, and my sense of call, I cannot spend the last day of vacation working.

I no longer return to church totally depleted with a side dose of guilt for not bringing my best self to worship on Sunday. It no longer hangs over my head the rest of the week and I don't struggle to build up momentum and get my head back into ministry. This change allows me to value myself and my time off, but it also enables me to value the integrity of the worship moment. It sets me up for success the whole following week and makes me more apt to use all of my vacation time because I am positively rewarding myself by seeing how a balance can be struck.

I earnestly believe that the most visible, impactful part of my job is leading worship. If I truly believe that, I need to treat each Sunday as important, but it is a toxic cocktail of arrogance and ego when I assume that the thing my congregation is longing for has to be my sermon on Sunday morning. If I'm not going to put in the full effort for that, as worship leader I need to create something else that can fulfill the same kind of spiritual longing they have. The people in the pews don't know I just got back from vacation. They are there because they are seeking, grieving, rejoicing, and looking to the church for something meaningful to connect with. If I can't be fully present, I need to support a worship experience that can help people make meaningful connections with God and community without my stress or tiredness getting in the way.

There is one idea to maximize time off that is untested in my ministry and feels quite extreme. It requires the utmost discipline and valuing of self and rest over work: write the sermon before I leave on vacation. Like, fully written, not an outline or good ideas or wishful thoughts: a manuscript sermon printed out, ready to go, and with just a few read-throughs required early on Sunday morning. I know. It's a wild idea! I'm not claiming to have done this, or that I ever will do it, but I hear rumors from the outer limits of my clergy circles that it is possible. Please report back to me if you do this with success.

Since I am not so bold or organized as to write a sermon in advance, I do the opposite: I do not preach at all. You read that right. I don't preach after vacation or professional time away. I have yet to figure out how to find the motivation to write a sermon a week or two in advance, so until that happens, I have sermon-alternatives that allow me to be fully present on my trip or staycation without carrying the seeds of a sermon in the back of my head, without trying to write a sermon on a cramped airplane with my seatmate adding in their commentary, without rushing a message the night before or in the wee early morning hours before worship.

Some of my alternatives may look like preaching to the congregation, but they are crafted in such a way that they can be prepared ahead of time and do not require the same kind of intense preparation that a traditional sermon requires. Other alternatives involve me leading worship but inviting someone else in the pulpit for the sermon or crafting a service that is not centered on a sermon. Regardless of how this looks in your setting, the focus is centering God and inviting people in to hear sacred stories in a new way.

TELL THE STORY

There are beautiful, long, detailed narratives throughout scripture that are truncated by our lectionary calendars or ignored all together. When we think of scripture as something to sit through before the sermon begins, we focus on the highlights of the story or pick parts that are easily digestible. When the sermon becomes the story, we are invited to hear scripture in a new way. Instead of a separate sermon, tell the story. Walk people through the book of Esther from Queen Vashti's bold refusal to Mordecai's eventual triumph. Take the journey with Jonah from the belly of the beast to Nineveh. On Transfiguration Sunday, don't start on top of the mountain with Jesus and the disciples, but detail the days before and follow them back down the mountain to see how that experience informed what came next. Be a storyteller. Draw out the details that bring the story to life and point out moments of connection to our own lives or highlight themes that speak to our faith.

There are a variety of ways to tell the story. Rewrite it in your own words. If it is a story you know deep in your bones, step out from the pulpit and tell it as you would sitting around a campfire. I love wordplay so I have sometimes transformed Bible stories into rhyming verses that help us listen in a new way or tap into our sense of playfulness in worship. Because we have a whole book of sacred stories to pull from, and because we have themes or a calendar throughout the year to rely on, this kind of preparation feels easier to do in advance. It is also the kind of energizing exercise I might do on a day when I have a spark of creativity and then save it for a Sunday that calls for a different kind of story.

WHAT DO YOU THINK?

My congregation, like all congregations, is full of people with a combined hundreds (thousands?) of years worth of wisdom. Often, they are waiting for someone to ask the right question, or any question, for them to share that wisdom. I love engaging my congregation in a sermon dialogue to tap into their wisdom, acknowledging that my sermonizing is just one source of Biblical interpretation. This is particularly powerful with stories that they know well, such as ones we tell every year like Jesus riding into Jerusalem on a donkey or Mary visiting Elizabeth when she is pregnant. There is an opportunity to step out of the pulpit and draw out the congregation to tell the story with you and fill in details they remember. You and the congregation can ask questions as the story is told. I might ask the congregation: what themes do you hear? How would you respond if Jesus said that to you? Do you see yourself in the crowd or as a disciple, and why? What stays with you from this passage? What feels challenging? The questions are endless.

Preparation involves an outline to guide the discussion and then enough trust to get you through the unknown of what might emerge when you ask: what do you think? The challenge and opportunity are to be comfortable with the unknown—you don't know what someone is going to share or what kind of answer they will give. As the dialogue facilitator, you have the opportunity to reframe their responses or push back if something is truly problematic, but every time my congregation has done this in a service, we are more often moved to collective wonder than we are discomfort. There are often moments of silence or seconds of awkwardness that feel like they will last forever, but if you can sit in the silence and trust that the awkwardness will transform into something else, there is power in hearing from the voices in the pews. There is power in making meaning together, in coming up with collective examples from our lives or the news, in working together to draw connections between scripture and our shared faith.

PRAY AND SING

Preaching and sermons are just one way to hear the word of God or connect our lived faith with an ancient story. In our worship services we incorporate multiple ways of entering into a sacred experience. It is possible to craft a service that explicitly focuses on the other ways we encounter God to the exclusion of a sermon. We can have a worship service where all we do is pray—in different ways, with different voices, on different themes, throughout the whole service. We can have a worship service where music is not just an interlude or transition to the next big thing, but it is the thing: short songs, new songs, favorite songs, soloists, choirs, special guests. We can shout out a hymn number and plan the arc of a music-focused service the way an artist might plan the arc of an album. Praying and music are forms of worship. They are strong enough and important enough to take center stage for a Sunday. Together we are called to pray and sing.

Planning this can be a collaborative effort. You might put out a call for musicians who wouldn't otherwise participate in weekly worship or invite your choir director to lead the service. You might do a poll of people's favorite hymns or ask if there is a worship song they know from another tradition that they might teach the congregation. If prayer is the focus, you can ask people what their favorite prayers are and if they might lead them with the congregation and share a time when that prayer was important to them. You can craft a service around the Lord's Prayer and ask for petitions based on each verse, opening up the service to sharing, silence, collective response, and room for the Holy Spirit to get a word in. Shifting the focus and rhythm of a service can be a source of comfort in the midst of grief or congregation transition—a way of acknowledging the deep feelings we don't always bring to the surface—or a source of deep energy and inspiration—shifting in such a way that moves people to gratitude for the practices your church shares and the space to dive deep into one aspect of worship. This can be done once a year or once a season, but as long as you do it with care and intention, people will hear the invitation to pray and sing.

LAY PREACHING

Because sermons are the center of the majority of worship experiences, it is helpful to have additional ways to cultivate different preaching voices. Even in congregations that have two or three pastors serving them, there is benefit to inviting other voices to the pulpit. Most mainline traditions believe that all members of the church are ministers and there are no restrictions on a lay member being called to preach. The only true restrictions requiring an ordained minister are related to sacrament. There is a gift in opening up preaching to members of the congregation, both to remind the church that your pastor does not have some hidden knowledge that is inaccessible to other people and to widen the perspectives and interpretations that are shared from the pulpit. Developing a lay preaching ministry is a win for clergy who can take breaks in their preaching and receive the gift of listening to someone else break scripture open, and a win for the congregation that sees their gifts celebrated in new ways.

My congregation has developed a lay preaching group that is self-sustaining. It is facilitated by a gifted writer and teacher in our congregation. I attended the first meeting where I talked about the structure of sermons and what makes a sermon different from an essay, and then they launched themselves into the life of the church. It is a group that supports each other from brainstorming ideas to acting as a writing group that gives feedback on drafts, to all showing up the day one of them is preaching to cheer and give delivery feedback. They regularly invite new members but after six years of working together, have a core team that each takes a turn preaching about once a year. At the beginning of the program year, I supply them with potential calendar dates and they create their own schedule.

Watching this group develop over the years has been a source of joy for the whole church. Core team members are now on their third or fourth sermon, and we have all watched their voices grow in strength and in their craft. What might start as a straightforward autobiographical reflection is now weaving in theology, stories, scripture, and beliefs. Because they develop their sermons through a group process, they are able to tackle big themes and tough topics. They have developed trust amongst one another and in their process of writing, editing, and revising, which allows them to hear critical feedback as well as be generous with their praise.

As a pastor, I love our lay preaching Sundays. I never take these Sundays as vacation days; it is important to be present to support this ministry. I move into the pews during the sermon and listen. Even though I may be leading other parts of the service such as the welcome and prayers, when I listen to a lay preacher, I feel like I am given an opportunity to fully worship. I always offer to meet with lay preachers ahead of time and give feedback on a draft. Meeting with lay preachers allows me to connect with them in a different way. Often, I witness them reveal new parts of themselves or their story, and it is a source of pride watching someone nervously step into the pulpit for the first time and be received by their church with encouragement and support. I love checking in after worship to see how they are feeling or what the experience was like.

Preaching is a craft that can be taught. It is a craft that involves study, prayer, writing, and public speaking. It is not a craft that requires a seminary degree but is best cultivated with practice. A pastor might begin a lay preaching program with one or two Sundays a year by directly asking people who they know have writing experience or a story to share with the congregation. It might be more directed by a pastor, working with a small group or with folks one-on-one. It is a ministry that takes intentional effort to initiate, but the benefits far outweigh that effort—even the effort of meeting with a group or individual preachers lends a different kind of energy and time than what you might spend preparing to preach each week.

There is one additional side effect to encouraging and developing lay preaching in your congregation: it gives the church an opportunity to support the pastor. Churches want to support their pastors, but often don't know how. As a solo pastor, I could easily preach forty-four or forty-six Sundays a year if I didn't create alternatives, not including funerals, weddings, and special weekday worship services. Every church member knows this is unsustainable or that even if I do eek out forty-four sermons, no one wins because surely some of those will be quite uninspired. They want to support their pastor in finding balance, but preaching and worship leadership seems like an area that is off limits unless the pastor gives explicit permission and support. After six years of solo pastoring and as many nurturing lay preaching, I received this email from the head of the lay preaching team:

I think our lay preaching team is large and experienced enough that we can handle about a sermon a month (maybe ten per year). Taking a small bit of pressure off you is one of the goals of the team, and I think it makes the work feel even more meaningful for all of us.

Who am I to deprive my generous, brilliant team a meaningful opportunity like freeing up their pastor ten extra weeks a year from the work of sermonizing? It would be downright unpastoral, and having seen the way this has become a core ministry in our congregation, I can't imagine my ministry without it.

These preaching alternatives do not have to wait for a return from vacation to happen. They can be incorporated throughout the year to break up your sermon writing, give you space to incubate new ideas, and allow more flexibility in how people are invited in to hear a sacred word. When we lean too hard into the idea that there is one person (or qualification) who is called to preach or one style of preaching, it becomes another way of thinking clergy are indispensable instead of remembering and celebrating all the ways God speaks to and through us and other people.

"NO" IS MY SAFE WORD

Some of the ways I have sought to prioritize time away and relaxing weekends doesn't have to do with changing the way I work or creating new programs. Some of the shifts are setting good-old-fashioned healthy boundaries. Often when we think about setting boundaries with people, we get hung up on what we are taking away. It feels like we are saying NO! in a way that leaves the other person dissatisfied and makes us feel like a meanie. Setting boundaries is also about saying YES! When you set a healthy boundary around your time, you are saying YES! to yourself as a person who deserves time away from work, YES! to the people, partners, friends, parents, and children in your life with whom you are called to be in relationship, and YES! to rest as renewal and restoration of your spirit and spirituality.

If you are walking around all the time and slinging out "No way! I don't have time for you!" in response to people's requests or invitations, all parties involved are going to feel like boundaries are punishment. But if creating boundaries around your weekend, or how many evenings you spend at the church, or whatever it is that needs a fresh boundary, means you are coming back more alive, more creative, and more able to be attuned to the pastoral concerns and problems of the parish, that is a major YES! for your ministry and everyone involved in it. The key is finding ways to say no that point toward a bigger yes—yes you want to support the person who is asking you about something, yes you want to support the many ministries of the church, and yes you are willing to work to find other ways to make things happen. Here are my top ten ways of gently saying no:

1. I'm honored, but no.
2. I'm not the right person for this project, but I have an idea about someone who is.
3. I need to turn down this opportunity, but keep me in mind in the future.
4. I am unavailable.
5. Thank you for asking but I don't have the bandwidth.
6. Let me think about it . . . Follow up later with: I've given it some thought and my answer is no.
7. I like this idea but now is not the right time to implement it—let's look ahead at the calendar.
8. For the pop-in "do you have a moment?" "No, but can we schedule that time to talk?"
9. I like your idea—here are some next steps to pursue before you circle back. Thank you for bringing this to my attention.
10. No.

Okay, sometimes no is just no. If Moses told God no five different times, hopefully you can take the risk of disappointing people every now and then. Sometimes a direct no—whatever the reason—is a reminder to folks that you are human and have limits. There are times when saying no can feel like a weight lifted off my shoulders. I get stressed out in advance—that discomfort with disappointing people is hardwired in me—but afterwards? When I know I am not agreeing to something that may cause me resentment or burnout or that I wouldn't have the capacity to do well? Relief. Deep sighs of gratitude that those two letters were invented so that they could come to my aid. You don't always need to give a reason. You don't have to make up an excuse. No is a holy word, and the more we use it, the less taboo it becomes and the more sacred it feels.

Saturday: Can This Really Work?

There are not many guarantees I'll make about leadership and ministry, but here is one: if you stay in the church long enough, there will come a time when everything that feels good and comfortable about your ministry is upended. You will feel like you have been knocked over by a tidal wave of stress, doubt, and grief. You will feel certain that you have made a horrible mistake and are called to do something else with your life. It might be something significant that upends your sense of call and comfort, but it is just as likely to be a thousand tiny moments stacked on top of each other that you don't notice until they knock you over. Even fantastic ministries with dreamy churches have days that feel impossibly difficult, days that stretch into entire seasons where you aren't sure you will ever make it out.

I have been there. More than once. Sometimes there is a concrete something to point to like a painful transition or upheaval that knocks me off my feet, or a global pandemic that knocks the whole church off its feet, and sometimes it has been a daily, lingering feeling that things aren't clicking the way they should. There are so many moving parts to tend to in ministry that occasionally they collide with each other, and my typical, well-paced week starts to feel out of control.

My other guarantee is that for ninety-nine percent of us, this will not be our last day in ministry. We'll get back up, probably fail a few more times, and then keep going. I am always in awe when I realize that has happened again—when it stops feeling like it is raining inside my office and instead feels like I can see a rainbow in the distance.

I have been able to go from shit's creek on Saturday to the sanctuary on Sunday morning by having a wider vision for ministry that is grounded in letting go, collaboration, and empowering lay leaders. Even in chaotic seasons, there are systems in place that keep conspiring to move myself and the church toward sustainability. There was once a time when I thought that if chaos reigned, it was going to be the new normal, but now I can acknowledge—and even lean into—the chaos, because I know that our systems of collaborative, laidback ministry will nudge their way back in and gradually transform the chaos into calm.

One of my many "rock bottom" moments (you thought there would only be one? You've got jokes!) caught me by surprise, because it was directly related to loving everything I was doing in ministry. As I settled into a new call and reached the end of my second year, I was feeling comfortable in the church. I felt like we really knew each other and were ready to think long-term and do some intentional growth. In my desire to transition my ministry from "new pastor" to "our pastor," I started saying yes to subcommittees we were forming to explore new ministry opportunities and yes to helping with programs we were dreaming up. Requests for one-on-one meetings increased as we started to live into our culture of "what if" and people wanted to brainstorm together or share their new ideas and passions before unleashing them in the church.

I said yes because I wanted to affirm these ideas and because I was excited about the future of the church. I kept squeezing in meeting after meeting, leaving no time in the day for general communications, worship planning, or the other things that get taken care of when you have a block of unscheduled time in the office. At the same time, because I was no longer the new pastor in town, I was getting invitations to join committees for my regional church conference and to collaborate with community partners. I wanted to build relationships and get to know my colleagues and community members, so I kept the YES! coming.

Before I knew it, I was spending most of my evenings at meetings instead of home and had a mountain of work I "had to catch up on" during my weekends. When I realized I hadn't caught my breath in weeks, when it felt like my to-dos were always longer than the things I got done, when my relationships became stressed because I didn't have the energy to be present emotionally anywhere except for work, I realized that old habits were back again. This was not new to me; it was just a new manifestation of old, familiar patterns.

Those old patterns brought up familiar feelings of being overwhelmed, depressed, and not wanting to do anything if it was just going to result in failure. I allowed myself about forty-eight hours to wallow in my misery before realizing that something was different this time. I could lean back on what I knew worked. I could reclaim the practices that were important to me. I knew that I could gracefully bow out of some commitments and still maintain collegial relationships. I could return to asking questions when someone asked to meet so that I would know what week to schedule the meeting for, recognizing that not every meeting needed to be scheduled the same week it was requested. I could return to blocking out portions of my week as office time, knowing that the solitary work I did there, or the work that bubbled up when I was present with staff during the day, was as much of value as the external or scheduled variety of ministry work.

I eased back into my laidback, collaborative, not-actually-about-me mode of ministry, making a few adjustments each week and not expecting perfection at any point in the process. The readjustments came quicker than expected because I wasn't inventing it as I was going along: I was relying on patterns that had already served me well and helped my ministry thrive. Returning to them felt comforting and familiar. They just needed intentionality and attention to resurface.

What is needed for success is a set of tools to ground your ministry and make it more sustainable. Many of these tools you have been carrying with you. Perhaps you forgot they were in your pocket. Perhaps they fell to the bottom of the pile as things stacked up around them. But they will be there when you need them. The goal is not to have perfect habits or a perfect ministry but tools and patterns you can lean into when you most need them. This is the part that takes months and years to cultivate, not just the attitude of, "I tried it once and I'm more stressed than ever." This is the part where I remind you that it did work, and it will work again.

OFF BALANCE FOR GOOD

Many years ago, I talked to my therapist about my frustration at not being able to find a balance in all aspects of my life from professional, home, health, and family of origin. For over a year I had been working on managing anxiety, managing time, saying no so I could say yes, and prioritizing the parts of my life that were most important to me. And still, I had weeks that felt impossibly overbooked and days that seemed like all I did was show up for the wrong thing or regret the decisions I made. I still got stressed out and tired and cranky. Wasn't all this intentional work and growth supposed to transform me?

I told my therapist, "I keep waiting for the day when I will find the perfect balance. There must be a formula that will allow me to balance work and home and my personal life in the perfect equation. Isn't that what growing up is about? When will that happen?" My therapist, who was typically reserved and serious, started laughing. Loudly. She almost fell out of her chair because she was shaking so hard from laughter. And then when she noticed I was in near tears, she pulled herself together and apologized.

She truly thought I was kidding, but I was sincere. What was the point of all this work if I couldn't master it one day? Why did I keep trying if I was ultimately going to fail? I felt like I was on a hamster wheel going nowhere, and I was ready to give up and hide in a corner for the rest of my life.

She explained that balance is a lie we teach ourselves and each other. Everything in our life shifts too often and too unpredictably for there ever to be sustained balance. One week your family might have an emergency and need more attention, so everything else has to adjust. Another week there might be several commitments at work or a pastoral crisis, and you have to find a way to make space for that while still doing the things that always have to be done like preparing for worship.

It's not about balance—it's about being nimble enough to shift and adapt as each day or week requires. If you start from a place of being overwhelmed, trying to adapt or shift feels more overwhelming and near impossible. But when you start from a place of strength, having a vision of the "non-negotiables" in your time, and what can give way to something more urgent, you are better able to live into the different needs of each week.

My therapist shifted me from an image of balance—a balance beam I was sure to eventually fall from—to imagining my life in terms of seasons. Some seasons are as bitter and unbearable as winter. But it is just a season. Some seasons are as warm and joy-filled as summer. Soak those up, because it is just a season. Know in the midst of the hard stuff that snow will melt and summer will return. We can't avoid a season. It will come. But we can be prepared. We can bundle up.

Living in Michigan, I quickly learned not to schedule something in the middle of winter without creating a snow date and advertising both dates together. Knowing that you're in a winter season, literally or metaphorically, requires having a Plan B you can turn to when it is needed. What is the way you can anticipate, navigate, and accept the inevitability of difficult seasons, knowing that even if you can't avoid them you can at least be equipped? And if you don't feel like you were best equipped this time, find the space to reflect on what you would have done differently *and then do it next time*.

I grew up in a mild Southern California climate so if you're reading the season analogy and it's not resonating for you, I totally get it. Solidarity. What image does work to help you understand that "this too shall pass"? When those old feelings or habits creep up on you (and if you're every bit as fallible as I am, they'll be back! I wrote this paragraph while avoiding the forty-seven emails that demanded a response) it is important to face them and to identify what specifically is the barrier. You can't transform if you don't know what you're changing.

Part of the foundation of my faith is hope, and I know I'm not the only one. I could retire early if I had a dollar for every clergy person that has Jeremiah 29:11 tattooed somewhere on their body: "For surely I know the plans I have for you, says the Lord, plans for your welfare and not for harm, to give you a future with hope." Hope is about knowing that there is more to come in our story, and that it is God guiding us.

Hope is important to hold onto when you hit a hiccup. Hope has a very close relationship to despair. We often do our best to turn away from despair or hide it from view instead of staring it in the face and challenging it. Hope comes from a place of despair—it comes when we transform the world as it is and imagine something new in its place.

When I look at the arc of the stories in the Bible, I am filled with hope because across the whole arc I can see how persistence, personal growth, and communal transformation are recurring themes. I see how each generation learns from the one that came before it. I see how it's never about one person's successes or failures and that there are always other people invited into the work of leadership, justice, and service. I see that I am not alone in longing to get it right, and not alone in feeling like a failure. Again: I see that I am not alone. We are not alone. You are not alone.

QUESTIONS FOR WHEN DESPAIR RETURNS

- Who are the trusted leaders in your congregation you can talk to?
- Who are the trusted colleagues you can talk to?
- Who are the people in your personal life (friends, family, chosen family, partners) you can talk to?
- Who are the trusted bishops or members of conference or regional leadership you can talk to?
- What tools do you have buried in your pocket to pull out and use?
- What does your vision for transformation look like?
- What does hope look like in this church?
- What does hope look like in your ministry?
- What was present the last time you felt joy?
- What do you need to access hope and joy again?

WHEN A PANDEMIC STRIKES (NOT A METAPHOR)

When I started writing this book, I'd had a decade of being an ordinary pastor serving ordinary churches during an ordinary time in history. None of the following phrases were a part of my regular vocabulary: social distancing, virtual worship, mitigating risk, work from home, and mandatory masks. Pivot was only to be used when making a joke about Ross from *Friends*. And yet, here I am, over two years deep into a global pandemic that has left most of the population homebound and the rest of the population risking their lives in service jobs interacting with the public.

Ministry in a world shaped by COVID-19—the seemingly unending variants, the constant shifting of plans or inability to create long-term plans, the high rates of illness and public health protections to navigate—is anything but ordinary. And while I ordinarily love my work and feel like ministry is the best job in the whole world, right now entire weeks are defined by longing for the way things were, grieving being separate from my people, and resenting the new normal that is sixty percent email communications, twenty percent Zooms, and twenty percent online worship.

Do you remember the time when technology was an afterthought for churches? When we were comically behind the curve for websites and barely considered having a social media presence? When many church pastors weren't given a laptop because working on a computer was an occasional necessity but never the focus of ministry, and certainly not something that needed to happen outside of the church office? Technology and having an online presence went from being an afterthought to our main mode of church life in a matter of days. The things that used to come easy—the informal conversations, facilitating large gatherings, being a visible presence in the community—

were categorized as high-risk behaviors and will feel unsafe for most of us for the foreseeable future.

Things have certainly changed. It's clear that the COVID-19 pandemic ushered in a seismic cultural shift that will impact what church looks like going forward. In the day-to-day, it is easy to dwell on the frustrations, losses, and challenges of being the church in a new era of ministry, but as I look back on these past few years, it is clear that many of the skills and values that made ministry the best of times are the same skills that have helped me continue to thrive in the most unpredictable of times. Conversely, the areas where I still have a lot of self-learning to do have become amplified and more urgent than ever. Being able to identify my personal growth areas in leadership equipped me to know what to look out for as my sense of "normal" fell apart.

In the before-times, one of my challenges was discerning my priorities when it often felt like there were dozens of tasks competing for time and attention, knowing that not all of them could possibly be accomplished. When the world shut down and churches had to pivot to an online model, there was instant clarity about what the most important tasks were. My church stopped trying to do it all. We dropped every single ball that we had been juggling and suddenly our church looked like a giant ball pit. Instead of diving in headfirst, we surveyed the landscape and actively decided which ministries were most important to lift back up.

We started with two ministries: worship and pastoral care. We quickly put all our resources and energy into creating an online worship experience that fit our congregation's needs. In those first few weeks, our congregation had no idea what to expect either, so we leaned into our culture of experimentation. We tried a few different models in the first few weeks, and then transitioned to slowly tweaking the model that worked best for us. Because we had a history of saying, "Let's try this out together," that language was translated into this new challenge without having to literally articulate it.

The work we had done together for the past few years of trying new ideas without the expectation that they would be The One Great Idea or wouldn't need adapting as we learned from our experiences paid off in this critical moment. Being able to say, "We're making this up as we go along but we'll keep trying until we find something that works" helped us find a sense of normal even as the tasks we were making up were brand new. Over and over, I received the message from church members that they didn't care about perfection. Rather, it was the ongoing effort and willingness to adapt to changing needs that they most appreciated.

There was also clarity about the increased need for pastoral care. Outreach wasn't just going to be for those who were sick or in crisis, but there was a whole new tier of folks who were about to become isolated or entrenched in a level of stress and uncertainty they had no preparation or support for. I knew I wasn't equipped to handle the increased pastoral care by myself; I already wasn't staying on top of the pastoral care needs in the before-time on my own. We assembled a team of folks to take on the responsibilities of calling folks, solicited names from the congregation as to who should be on the list, and got to work. For years we have been moving to a model of congregational care instead of the pastor as caretaker, so this was our opportunity to flex that muscle.

This time of crisis didn't slow down my ideas about what the church should be doing, but it clarified how limited my time was. Change is exhausting and when I tried to stretch myself too thin, the stress, exhaustion, and insomnia that followed was worse than in the before-times.

I'm grateful I practiced turning down my own ideas and listening for what others are equipped to do. This was a season where every Zoom or call I was on, someone inevitably asked,

"How can I help out in the church?" There wasn't a time to do a gifts/interests survey with the congregation, but instead was a time to identify the needs and let folks respond as they felt called. The less I did, the more I let go, the more empowered my people were. They were clearly looking for ways to find meaning and feel helpful during this time. It felt sinful for me to over-function and try to control how we responded as a community or how things should be done.

Similarly, those relationships of collaboration that I'd built became lifesaving sources of support and idea sharing. Bringing our faith communities together made them feel like they were part of something larger than our little, lonely church. Thanks to a music director who happened to have a tech background, my church got really good, really fast at virtual choirs. When colleagues started sharing how they struggled to integrate music into worship, we uploaded our choir pieces as individual videos online and invited our sister churches to use them as needed. It cost us nothing in time or money to share.

We also invited other churches to join our choir and add their voices to ours, which allowed our congregations to see that they were not alone and could build relationships without even being in the same room together. There was a spirit of generosity that triumphs over the spirit of competition. It was a great opportunity to lean into our gifts in the knowledge that we would be looking to other congregations to fill gaps we wouldn't be able to do ourselves. No one congregation is The Church of All Things. I hope we continue to work together to bring the best of ourselves to share with our neighbors.

I name these successes as a reminder for myself more than for anyone else because day in and day out this period of time felt impossibly challenging. One of my skill sets is listening to the congregation, during informal conversations and formal meetings, to get the pulse of the congregation, anticipate needs, and craft our vision for whatever season we are living in.

I hadn't realized how much of that listening work was dependent on being in-person. It seems that spatial presence was a precondition for my ability to feel the energy in the room, and certain connections only seem to happen when there is space for conversation to wander, when there is an ability to continue talking once a meeting has been adjourned or in those spare minutes before the official business begins. Even though I heard from folks on emails and saw them on countless Zooms each week, I was cut off from the beating pulse of the church, which made me feel like I didn't know what we were doing or what our overall purpose during this extended crisis was.

I was able to mitigate the underlying feeling of disconnection by leaning into our communication systems, posing direct questions at every turn, and trusting the answers I received. I tried to separate the expressions of anxiety from reality to assess where we were as a congregation and how we might be called to respond as a church in a new season. Check-ins were no longer just about personal wellbeing (although that was also even more critical), but required asking what people thought was important for the church to be focusing on, or how they saw us living out our mission. The questions that we might ask during a time of strategic planning were once again relevant and needed to shape these COVID-19 years where none of us had any clue what we are supposed to be doing and we were all just making it up as we went along.

Personally, I felt challenged as a pastor because when the physical building of the church shut down and everything became suspended or moved online, my work week revolved around tedious tasks and email that multiplied in volume. Suddenly there were no more opportunities to show up and sit in the back of the room during a program, no more potlucks where the only requirement was my attendance. Now, even meetings demanded novel forms of strategizing as we balanced new dynamics and group norms online. Instead of looking at my calendar for the day so that I could show up and improvise (I think the professional term is "ministry of presence"), suddenly I had hard deadlines with a lot of prep work and planning to execute. It felt like week after week I was running from one deadline to the next, trying to squeeze in the emails that had multiplied because it was suddenly the only way we were communicating.

At the same time, our collective sense of time slipped away as our wall calendars became decorations and the days blended together due to the monotony of our routines. Those hard-fought and precious boundaries I had around time off and weekends slipped away as I tried to assemble a pre-recorded worship service and the steep learning curve kept me working through Friday night and well into Saturday, making the weekend obsolete.

There were more tasks to accomplish than there were hours in the day and days in the week. I had to follow suit with my congregation and get really clear about what I could and could not spend time doing. It meant renewed honesty and upfront conversations about how I was spending my time and what I had the bandwidth to accomplish.

When outdoor worship became a safe way to gather, someone suggested we do them once a week, responding to the yearning each of us felt to be gathered together, even in a small group, even six to eight feet apart. I replied gently: "If you want me to lead these services, I can lead one in the next month. Adding an additional weekly service will quickly burn me out." So, we started with one. And that was enough.

I felt nervous about reinforcing boundaries around my time, but because I was clear about my limits, my congregation responded from a place of love and acceptance. It helped that no one had time for passive aggression or pettiness in the midst of a global crisis that was playing out in every single one of our homes. It turned out this was the perfect time to be strong about your boundaries with time off and expectations about how much you would take on. Culturally, we had a renewed awareness that everyone has different needs.

Even when my anxiety dragon reared its head and I worried I would disappoint people or not live up to their ideal of what a pastor should be, when I stayed authentic to what I needed and communicated that clearly and often, I felt heard and respected. We were on the same team, and church members were negotiating their needs and desires as much as I was. The more we practiced, the easier these negotiations became.

What I have learned is that a crisis does not create change in the system so much as it exacerbates what is already there. If there are areas that are weak and need attention, they might feel hopelessly broken in the face of a pandemic. If there are areas where your church naturally excels, those will fall into place in new ways. Crisis creates extremes and stress is inevitable. Instead of panicking and feeling like I had to reinvent ministry, I leaned into what worked well and let that take care of itself (or let my church members take care of it, more accurately) and tended to the parts that needed assistance. These were the same things that needed tending to in the best of times, they just felt easier to ignore when the world wasn't falling apart on our doorstep.

If you stay in ministry long enough, I guarantee there will be a time when everything falls apart. But here is the Good News: you are not alone. Not now, not ever. There is a church at work beside you. There are colleagues who share the same struggles. There are people who have walked this road who will guide you now. You are equipped exactly as you are. You have the experience, the wisdom, and past successes to know how to adapt and begin again. You are enough.

Sunday: Get to Work

If you've made it this far, one of three things has likely happened:

1. You have contemplated ways to shift your ministry or church culture to create a workload that feels more balanced and aligned with values that believe you should have life outside of work. If that is you, welcome!
2. You have started making changes or planting seeds with other folks at church about how to ensure the life of the church does not gravitate around you. If that is you, you are also welcome.

3. You skipped ahead to the last chapter because you're skeptical and you want to see how it all turns out. You, too, are welcome here.

It's Sunday, people! Time to get to work! You've spent all week offloading your responsibilities onto your congregation and finding collaborators to share the burden with you. Now the fun begins. When your work as a pastor is to amplify the vision of the church and empower the body of Christ to live it out, Sunday is the only day you really work.

When we show up for worship on Sunday morning, week after week, it becomes the norm for us and we start to take it for granted. We forget what a unique opportunity it is. This is the moment the whole community is gathered together. How many organizations can say they are able to gather all their supporters not just once a year or via a newsletter, but every single week in the flesh or on a live Zoom call? Sunday morning is an opportunity to share the vision of the church, to affirm all the ministry your church members are doing, and to inspire them to follow Jesus.

Folks show up for worship on Sunday morning looking for many different things: comfort from grief, a sense of belonging, affirmation that they are loved, purpose in their life, connection with community, free coffee. Embedded in each of these desires is a longing for their lives to be impacted in a positive way. They hope, and even expect, that being a part of the church, especially on Sunday morning, will change their lives. People who show up on Sunday already have a seedling of faith planted in them, and they are looking for nutrients to help it grow.

There are moments when these hopes feel like a lot of pressure, especially knowing that each person is bringing a different expectation. There are moments when I start to internalize that old idea that I need to be all things to all people, or that it is my responsibility to create a Sunday morning experience in worship and beyond that speaks deeply to everyone. It's not like we have different worship services that cater to each person's needs. Worship necessitates a "one size fits most" approach, so as the pastor, it is my responsibility to craft a service that is clear in what it says but leaves enough space that people can write their own stories into it.

There are Sunday mornings when that feels like a daunting task—particularly when I am still drained from over functioning and micromanaging the whole week before. I have had Sunday mornings when I just want to get through to the other side, when I hope that so-and-so who is a pain in the you-know-what doesn't show up because I don't have spare energy, when I feel like I don't have anything meaningful to share. To be honest, Sunday morning is most daunting when I haven't gotten my own needs met during the rest of the week such that I can't shift my focus outside of myself. Writing that makes me say "ouch" in its honesty, but it is also a good reminder that what we do Monday through Friday impacts how we show up on Sunday.

It's hard to name these feelings, even long after the fact, even though I know I am not alone in my insecurities, because they carry a veil of shame with them. When I'm defensive or depleted I start to resent the expectations that people bring with them. My depletion doesn't have to do with who is there that Sunday or not, it doesn't have to do with the wording of a particular prayer or the way the anthem flows with the sermon or if the post-worship snacks are delicious enough. It has to do with my spiritual and emotional capacity to be open to receiving whatever the Holy Spirit and ordinary people bring into the sanctuary with them.

I am not proud of feeling this way, but it is always a reflection of my own well-being, clarity of vision, and spiritual readiness. It might feel like external pressure and forces are creating the doubts or separating me from the worship moment, but when I follow the threads leading to my biggest doubts or defensiveness or insecurity, they are directly related to how rested and prepared I am that day, how connected I am to the vision of the church, and how much of the Sunday experience has been a collaborative effort.

There will never be a perfect Sunday. Have I said it enough that perfection is not the goal? If you find yourself seeking perfection, channel Jesus and say: "Get behind me Satan!" There will be breathtaking moments when Sunday flows from a week where you have successfully lived out the vision and empowered the people in the pews to Be the Church; moments that pastors bear witness to and can worship God through because we are not responsible for them. They're the moments when we've moved out of the way long enough to let the Holy Spirit be the agent and actor.

Sunday morning work is about being as clear as possible about what the church is and what the church isn't. It is about helping every person present find their place in the church and a connection to God in their life. And pastors are off the hook because if someone has come into the building, chances are they are hoping to make that happen as well.

Secular organizations would kill for the opportunity to get all of their stakeholders in a room together every single week, share their vision, and ask them to commit to living out that vision together. How many times do we take this for granted? How many times do we feel so exhausted by trying to do it all ourselves that we miss the power in giving it away and sharing with our siblings in Christ?

WORSHIP READINESS

Worship is most successful when I start thinking about it as early as possible and bring as many collaborators as possible into the room. Some weeks this is just staff—getting my bulletin to my administrator early enough that the proofreaders have time to change "Come Though Font" to "Come Thou Fount."

It means picking hymns with enough time that my organist can remind me that for the past six years I have started Advent with the same hymn no one knows except me and perhaps we'd like to try a different one this year? It means naming a theme or focus scripture early enough that whoever is doing the children's message can go through their own brainstorming process or we can appropriately schedule mission moments and lay announcements for the appropriate week. Due to my poor planning, a church member once had to give a rousing "come be silly with us at Trunk or Treat" invitation immediately after a two-hanky sermon on loss and death. Oops. No one was in the mood for that invitation, and it could have been avoided if I had spent more time thinking about the flow and goals of the service instead of just saying yes to a special announcement and plugging it in where it always goes.

I am not a pastor who sets aside a week in the summer to plan the whole worship year ahead with spreadsheets and flip charts and cross-referenced worship resources. That experiment lasted as long as maintaining one to-do list. I am conscious about what parts of worship are helpful to do in advance and I try to disseminate that information several weeks in advance: major themes, departures from the lectionary, any guest preachers or different styles of worship. Other parts can happen week to week, like developing the order of worship and creating liturgy.

(By creating liturgy, I mean finding and crediting people whose skill it is to write liturgy—there are many books and blogs where writers encourage congregations to use their liturgy with attribution. Finding the perfect prayers that someone else has written, rather than writing my own, helps me dive into the themes of each service without feeling the pressure of making everything original or in my own voice. Writing liturgy is a skill that is low on my priority list, and I am thankful there are ample resources from gifted writers to pull from.)

The mix of working ahead and preparing for the week helps me hold worship in my head in the days leading up to Sunday. My sermon starts marinating as early as Monday and then I craft my manuscript on Thursday. I do not schedule meetings on Thursday past noon so that I have uninterrupted time to write. I tend to write at home where there are fewer interruptions, or at my favorite coffee shop where I have an eight o'clock deadline when they close. Setting that deadline gives me a hard stopping point, and because I left my day open, I always leave with a completed manuscript and a piece of pie to take home as my reward.

After Thursday, I breathe. I do not think about worship on Friday, when I can relax, feeling confident that everyone has what they need to co-lead the service and I have my sermon finished. On Saturday, at some point during the day, I will take fifteen minutes to read through my sermon and make any minor edits. By that point I have prepared for worship bit by bit throughout the week such that I can feel the rhythm of the service the same way I can feel my heartbeat. It becomes second nature—not too controlled, but to the point that I can trust that the necessary elements have been thoughtfully prepared by myself and others such that there is space for the Holy Spirit to fill in the rest. This is my gold standard, which isn't to say it happens exactly this way every week. But the more I practice spreading the worship preparation and sermonizing across the week, the more routine it feels.

SUNDAY FROM START TO FINISH

Real talk: my best Sundays are ones where I'm not waking up to slap a conclusion on my sermon, but am instead waking up relaxed, knowing there is no work I need to do before I arrive at the church. I feel best when I start Sunday early in the morning by doing something for myself: walking my dog, watching a few sketches from last night's *SNL* episode, whatever feels indulgent and clears my head. A more pious person than me might say they recommend an hour of meditative prayer each Sunday morning, but to me that sounds like an extra hour of sleep. Your mileage may vary.

I am intentionally not the first person to arrive at the church on Sunday morning. This reminds me that other folks are as responsible for the church as I am, even on Sunday morning, and we are each doing our part to pull together worship. I arrive and hide in my office for half an hour looking through the bulletin, reading my sermon, and making sure there are not any new emails or voicemails about pastoral care concerns that need to be woven into the prayers. All other email and communication waits until Monday.

I do a walkthrough of the church, saying hello and thanking all the volunteers and staff who are already working: folks in the kitchen brewing coffee or by the front door waiting to greet people; our new member volunteer ready with fresh nametags and information folders; the head usher setting up the sanctuary; teachers reviewing their lesson plans; the choir rehearsing. I answer any questions that need answering or ask the questions I have.

These moments are my favorite of the week. Everyone in the building has a purpose and knows their role. We work side by side to turn our building into a church, bringing ministry to life through hospitality and worship, paying attention to the details that make a big difference. Not including the choir, there are at least fifteen volunteers every Sunday morning who work together to create church. These responsibilities are seen as shared, and we thrive on Sunday morning because no one claims any role for themselves.

I do not pay attention in advance to who our Sunday morning volunteers are; I wait to encounter whoever is in each role. It is not uncommon for someone to let me know they are filling in at the last minute for someone who is ill or to watch someone step in and begin a task when they realize no one else has started. When I finally make my way to the sanctuary, I look in the bulletin to see who my worship leader is, and then keep an eye out for them to arrive and check in. If they don't arrive and the service begins, I barely have a second to panic because several other people have kept their eye out for the worship leader and if they haven't seen them either, someone slides beside me behind the pulpit and says they would be happy to do the job. Even I'm dispensable! On a memorable Maundy Thursday service, a service with a lot of words to get through, a tickle in my throat turned into a coughing fit and a church member came forward and picked up where I left off in the manuscript. It does not benefit anyone for me to have sole ownership over worship.

Releasing these details to the community by modeling my own willingness to let go, and encouraging them to do the same, frees me up to be present in other ways. I introduce myself to the early arrivers who are inevitably visitors because all of the regulars are running in as service begins. I sit and listen to the choir rehearse, letting their anthem penetrate my spirit in a way that will be more difficult in the midst of facilitating worship. I try to connect with people I pass in the hallway, setting the tone for the morning. Most of all I wait. I wait for the prelude to begin, the people in the pews to quiet, and worship to start.

There are different philosophies about worship that touch on matters such as what elements are most important and how to best get there. One of my guiding principles as a curator and facilitator of worship is to ensure that people are not just experiencing worship as it happens to them, but are a part of bringing worship to life. If after sixty minutes it has been solely focused on me and my words, I feel like something significant is missing, even if I had the best words to share. It is important to give everyone in attendance the opportunity to bring worship to life and to help orient our spirits toward a sacred experience.

We have built parts into our liturgy that help us do this: responsive or unison prayers and singing together are the main two. Those are the familiar pieces that let people settle in and practice using their voices so that they can be prepared to be invited to do something additional. A children's sermon that is a call and response with the whole congregation, a variation on the pastoral prayer that invites folks to pray for one another with their bodies or by crying out together. A new way to add voices, movement, writing, or artistic expression into our praise of God, to help congregants see that this moment of glory needs each of us, that every voice and body and expression matters, that they made a difference by being there today. This foundational principle carries over from worship across every aspect of ministry. I've never had someone leave worship and say, "Because of what we did here, I'm going to step into a new leadership role!" But I have had people leave worship saying that the experience was going to follow them into the rest of the week.

People do not want to just consume worship or be the consumers of the church. We are co-creators. Sunday is the opportunity to spread this message of co-creation to every person in the church, whether it is their first time or their five-hundredth time attending. Everyone has a role to play, and no one is more important than the next. What an opportunity to affirm and uplift all the gifts that are present. What an opportunity to name the mission of the church and lift up the shared vision.

THAT'S ALL, FOLKS

I have come a long way from the burnout and depression that left me avoiding church and in fear of leaving ministry. There are still times when I feel the threat of overwhelm-too-much-can't-say-no start to take over. When that happens, I have a higher awareness of what is bubbling up for me. I can see the choices I've made that lead to stress, and the more I practice, the more often I am able to slow down enough to see where my choices will lead me and perhaps even make a different choice. Letting go, collaborating, and focusing on empowering and equipping lay leaders has created a foundation that is sustainable and makes me feel like it is possible to be a pastor and thrive.

Pastors are not alone in this work. We are part of a congregation that longs to do this work with us. There might be three of them. There might be thirty. There might be 3,000. But they are there. The best ministry happens when we are learning together, experimenting together, even failing together. The key part is together.

When I dreamed of being a pastor in a church, I would play the scene from *The Lion King* where Mufasa shows their land to his son Simba and says, "Everything the light touches is our kingdom." Except in my fantasy, I changed it to "Everything is *my* kingdom." It turns out that the scene only works if the whole lion pride is surveying the land together and says, "This is *God's* kingdom." The church doesn't belong to me. The church is not a reflection of me. There are parts of being the church that are my responsibility, and there are many other parts that are not. The clearer I am about those distinctions, and the more I can cultivate my own identity and sense of self outside of my role as a pastor, the more the church thrives and the more I thrive.

Sunday morning, after a week of delegating and letting go and encouraging others, is a celebration of all we do together. It symbolizes the work of the church by the people of the church. It is a time of gratitude and reflection, and it gives us courage to begin again. My hope is that on Sunday morning, as with the rest of the week, we can slow down and draw our awareness to all the parts of the congregation moving together to create something that is bigger than any one of us.

Acknowledgments

Writing this book was a group effort from start to finish. The idea first sparked from a beloved church member, Alice, who was a partner in ministry and taught me so much about effective leadership. She once told me, "You have a book somewhere inside you." It took me several years to believe her, but I never forgot that first nudge. Everything in this book is a result of listening to and learning from my best ministry mentors—church members.

Thank you to all the moderators, vice-moderators, committee members, Sunday morning volunteers, staff, and anyone who has ever said "yes" to serving in a church. You have seen the best and worst of what the church can be and do, and you keep showing up for the love of God and God's people anyway.

My laidback ministry practices and philosophies took root in two incredible congregations: The Congregational Church of South Glastonbury in Connecticut and Edgewood United Church of Christ, UCC in East Lansing, MI. Thank you for making ministry feel like joyful play. Thank you for failing exuberantly with me on occasion and still being willing to try new things. Thank you for leading with love in all that we do together. You make me feel like I have the best job in the whole world.

Ministry formation doesn't begin with ordination or a paid position. I am indebted to the First Congregational Church of Bakersfield, UCC and Hancock United Church of Christ in Lexington, MA for the ways you each shaped me as a youth and young adult seminary intern. Your lay leaders encouraged and nurtured my gifts, and helped me find my voice when I wasn't sure I had anything worthwhile to say.

Thank you to my clergy colleagues and clergy mentors who provide a soft place to land on hard days and celebrate every win with wild enthusiasm. Thank you especially to Betsy, Alice, and Kit for all the time at the table together, and to Phiwa for our coffee shop conversations.

Speaking of coffee shops, they have been both sanctuary and fertile ground for me while writing this book. Foster Coffee, Blue Owl, Chapelure, Strange Matter, Hooked, Mitten Raised, Grand Traverse Pie Co.—thank you for holding space for our community and keeping me caffeinated.

Thank you to Collegeville Institute for the ways you transformed my understanding of vocation through the Communities of Calling Initiative.

Thank you to The Pilgrim Press, especially Rachel and Katie, for your investment in first time authors and your persistent nudges to keep going. Thank you to the Phoenix cohort for the creative space and mutual sharing of our hopes and dreams as writers.

Thank you to my family, especially Mom and Brian, for a lifetime of support and love, and for passing on your wicked sense of humor.

Thank you to Beth, whose deep well of encouragement and love there are simply not enough words to express. Thank you for always being my idea incubator, first reader, and early editor. Thank you for challenging me to be my most authentic self and for making home my favorite place to be. You claim not to like group projects, but I can't imagine a better partner to build a life with.

Acknowledgments

[illegible]

[illegible]

[illegible]